I0758715

SOUTH CAROLINA 1720 JURY LIST

Copyright 2 March 2021
Stemmons Publishing
1078 Shields Lane
South Jordan, Utah 84095

INTRODUCTION

1010-SOUTH CAROLINA 1720 JURY LIST This publication has 840 entries covering a time when South Carolina was only 50 years old and the population was very small with only an estimated 885 heads of household. Unfortunately, it does not list a residence other than South Carolina. For information on how to obtain this book search by the title or "Books by John Stemmons" at Amazon.com. This comes automatically with a paperback binding.

South Carolina has a remarkable series of records that makes it unique for the Colonial period. These are the "Jury Lists" compiled by the government to function as a list of names from which members of a jury could be assigned. They cover the period 1720-1783 and, according to the act in 1731, were compiled from tax lists of the preceding year (which unfortunately no longer exist), listing every person who paid a tax of twenty shillings or more. Those who paid five pounds, or more were listed as grand jurors. The poorer class of people would not be listed. While not a complete list of the heads of household, they represent a sizeable proportion. They serve as a census during a period of growth, migration, and war. Usually only the name and residence is given (the 1720 list does not give residence), but sometimes an occupation or name of the father is listed, etc. Many names are on more than one list for a particular year. *South Carolina 1720 Jury List* contains 840 entries for a very early period in South Carolina's history.

In 1720, South Carolina's white population was estimated to be about 9,000 and using the 1790 household size of 5.5 persons[1] there would be approximately 1,636 households. Ignoring duplicates, this book includes about 51% of the households in South Carolina at that time. Of course, counting the duplicate names would make the percent smaller.

It is suggested that those using this book read through the section containing the text of the act that was passed.

Also helpful is the "Guidelines for Entry of Names" section.

The originals of these records are at the South Carolina Department of Archives and History.

Grateful appreciation is extended to the South Carolina Department of Archives and History for their kind assistance in obtaining copies of these records.

SOUTH CAROLINA

1720 JURY LIST ACT NO. 422

An Ordinance Passed by ye General Assembly June 11th 1720.

It is hereby Ordered by the present General Assembly, that the Several Persons whose Names are mentioned in the Several Lists hereunto Annexed, as Grand Petite Jurymen, be and are hereby appointed to Serve as Such, your servant to the Several Acts in that case made and provided. Ja. Moore, [name unreadable] [The previous text is not included in the published version of this act, but is in the original document at the South Carolina State Archives .]

In the published version of this act we find the following:

AN ORDINANCE of the General Assembly for settling the Jury Lists.

(Passed June 11, 1720. As this consists only of lists of names, I have not thought it necessary to copy it.)

---

[1] Department Of Commerce and Labor, Bureau of the Census, *A Century Of Population Growth From The First Census Of The United States To The Twelfth, 1790-1900* (Washington, D.C.: Government Printing Office, 1909), 7, 96.

(Cooper, Thomas, M.D.-L.L.D., *The Statutes at Large of South Carolina; Edited, Under Authority of the Legislature, Volume Third, Containing the Acts from 1716, Exclusive, to 1752, Inclusive. Arranged Chronologically.* Printed by A. S. Johnston, 1838. page 111.)

INDEXES

Indexes are expensive to compile.
Which is why many books do not have them. Most that do just have a simple name index. A noteworthy exception is the *Territorial Papers of the United States* which gives some limited context as explained below.
Indexes are expensive but using modern technology we at Stemmons Publishing have included nearly all the context you may need. 100% context is probably not possible such as in a census that lists multiple neighbors. Search for entries of the same page in our book(s) or the original document if you require more information.

PUBLICATIONS FROM STEMMONS PUBLISHING

These following publications are not just traditional alphabetical lists of names, they include the context of information with each name!!

Why is that so important? Because many of the names in our books were obtained from various sources including South Carolina jury lists, the *Territorial Papers of the United States* (28 volumes each with its own index), petitions, tax lists, etc., and like most books with indexes common names require a lot of time to check each entry in the index. Can you imagine how many Smiths you would have to go through page-by-page for a compilation the size of *Territorial Papers of the United States*? Their indexes provide some context such as signing a petition. No explanation is given of what, when, or why the petition was made. Because we have included the context with each name, you can easily search all the Smiths, Taylors, Browns, Williams, etc., without all the drudgery! And since most of us have common surnames, we may need some help. Now, the originals of the South Carolina jury lists are housed in the South Carolina Department of Archives and History. Therefore, you may not have access to the originals. The way we index names means it is almost as good as being at the Archives yourself and doubly so since these documents are loose papers and do not have an original index. Our books provide an enhanced way of using *Territorial Papers of the United States* that the original compilers did not envision. So, if you have this collection, your obtaining our books compiled from those volumes will help your access to *Territorial Papers of the United States* even if you are not interested in our books about South Carolina jury lists. Now, that's what I call achieving the potential of a real index! It takes the bare skeleton of a name on a list and covers it with the flesh, hair, eyes, etc., of a human body. The names are more able to stand alone by themselves than is the case with a traditional index. We did not index subjects. *Territorial Papers of the United States* did.

Checking a name from our books and going to the page in *Territorial Papers of the United States* will show the list of names. Those listed next to the person of interest may be neighbors and relatives.

Guidelines for Entry of Names

Many times, names have been difficult to decipher. Other times, the document itself has been damaged in various ways that impacted our ability to read the information. Several methods have been employed to indicate to the reader when we had difficulty. They are as follows:

1. When a surname has been difficult to determine and could be read alternately, we have indicated this by using two and sometimes three possibilities. For example, Rud or Ried. For your convenience we have made separate entries for each possibility: Rud or Ried and Ried or Rud. We encourage individuals to go to the original source and make a determination for themselves if the name is important for their research. For given names, we will also indicate more than one possibility, but will not make separate entries for each one.

2. When an undetermined number of letters were unreadable, we used the ellipsis ". . ." in place of the letters we could not decipher, while we included those characters we could read. For example: Cr . . . [surname] and . . . seph [given name]. It would be difficult to determine the surname with confidence, but the given name is most likely "Joseph".

3. When a known number of characters could not be read, an asterisk "*" was used in place of each letter we could not decipher. Often the name can be determined based on where the asterisk is placed. For example, with Brow* one can readily determine the name is most likely Brown. However, when one or more asterisks are placed at the beginning of a name, the possibilities become more numerous and therefore difficult to determine.

4. When we were unsure about the reading, we would include a question mark "?" after the name.

5. Sometimes we could not read the name because the writing was too faint, it was covered with ink blotches, portions of the document was damaged/missing, or for many other reasons. We tried to indicate this when we felt a name was there by using "[Unreadable]", "[Missing]", "[Illegible]", "[Name crossed out]", etc., in place of the name. In some cases, a name might be read by examining carefully the original document. If individuals are successful in deciphering the name, the compilers would appreciate receiving feedback from them indicating what the name should be.

6. When the first letter was obviously wrong and would interfere in a researcher's ability to readily see the name, we have placed in brackets what we thought the name should be along with the spelling of the name in the original. One can use the search feature on the Internet to find these names. An example is Knewkurk [Newkirk], Richard. A researcher might never know to look under the spelling Knewkurk and therefore miss potentially vital information. By searching for the name Newkirk, one would find this entry.

7. Sometimes it is difficult to tell which is the given name and which is the surname. When there has been doubt about the proper order of given name/surname, we have made an entry such as: Everet or Jones, [surname], and Jones or Everet [given name]. Then we have made another entry with the names reversed such as Jones or Everet [surname], and Everet or Jones [given name].

When deciphering entries, we have always tried to err on the side of reasonable, known, practical, and possible names rather than unreasonable, impossible, or impractical spellings.

SOUTH CAROLINA 1720 JURY LIST

There are 840 entries.

ACALE, Robt, - He is on the "Petite" Jury list.- *Jury Lists, 1720, Acts #422, [at South Carolina Archives]*, pg. 12.
Acale, Robt, Male

ACHBY, Jno, - He is on the "Petite" Jury list.- *Jury Lists, 1720, Acts #422, [at South Carolina Archives]*, pg. 14.
Achby, Jno, Male

ACHBY, Thos, - He is on the "Petite" Jury list.- *Jury Lists, 1720, Acts #422, [at South Carolina Archives]*, pg. 14.
Achby, Thos, Male

ADAMS, Wm, - He is on the "Petite" Jury list.- *Jury Lists, 1720, Acts #422, [at South Carolina Archives]*, pg. 10.
Adams, Wm, Male

ADAMS, Wm, - He is on the Grand Jury list.- *Jury Lists, 1720, Acts #422, [at South Carolina Archives]*, pg. 2.
Adams, Wm, Male

ADDAMS, Wm, - He is on the "Petite" Jury list.- *Jury Lists, 1720, Acts #422, [at South Carolina Archives]*, pg. 5.
Addams, Wm, Male

AKENS, Jams, - He is on the "Petite" Jury list.- *Jury Lists, 1720, Acts #422, [at South Carolina Archives]*, pg. 11.
Akens, Jams, Male

AKINS, Jno, - He is on the "Petite" Jury list.- *Jury Lists, 1720, Acts #422, [at South Carolina Archives]*, pg. 11.
Akins, Jno, Male

AKINS, Thos, - He is on the "Petite" Jury list.- *Jury Lists, 1720, Acts #422, [at South Carolina Archives]*, pg. 14.
Akins, Thos, Male

ALLEN, Wm, - He is on the "Petite" Jury list.- *Jury Lists, 1720, Acts #422, [at South Carolina Archives]*, pg. 6.
Allen, Wm, Male

ALLIN, Thos, - He is on the "Petite" Jury list.- *Jury Lists, 1720, Acts #422, [at South Carolina Archives]*, pg. 13.
Allin, Thos, Male

ALSTON, Jno, - He is on the "Petite" Jury list.- *Jury Lists, 1720, Acts #422, [at South Carolina Archives]*, pg. 11.
Alston, Jno, Male

ALSTON, Wm, - He is on the "Petite" Jury list.- *Jury Lists, 1720, Acts #422, [at South Carolina Archives]*, pg. 10.
Alston, Wm, Male

ARDEN, Edward, - He is on the "Petite" Jury list.- *Jury Lists, 1720, Acts #422, [at South Carolina Archives]*, pg. 8.
Arden, Edward, Male

ARMSTRONG, Chas, - He is on the "Petite" Jury list.- *Jury Lists, 1720, Acts #422, [at South Carolina Archives]*, pg. 6.
Armstrong, Chas, Male

ASH, Richd, - He is on the "Petite" Jury list.- *Jury Lists, 1720, Acts #422, [at South Carolina Archives]*, pg. 5.
Ash, Richd, Male

ASPINELL, Jno, - He is on the "Petite" Jury list.- *Jury Lists, 1720, Acts #422, [at South Carolina Archives]*, pg. 10.
Aspinell, Jno, Male

ATWELL, Benja, - He is on the "Petite" Jury list.- *Jury Lists, 1720, Acts #422, [at South Carolina Archives]*, pg. 6.
Atwell, Benja, Male

ATWELL, Josph, Junr, - He is on the "Petite" Jury list.- *Jury Lists, 1720, Acts #422, [at South Carolina Archives]*, pg. 6.
Atwell, Josph, Junr, Male

ATWELL, Josph, Senr, - He is on the "Petite" Jury list.- *Jury Lists, 1720, Acts #422, [at South Carolina Archives]*, pg. 6.
Atwell, Josph, Senr, Male

BACCOT, Petr, - He is on the "Petite" Jury list.- *Jury Lists, 1720, Acts #422, [at South Carolina Archives],* pg. 8.

Baccot, Petr, Male

BACON, Michael, - He is on the "Petite" Jury list.- *Jury Lists, 1720, Acts #422, [at South Carolina Archives],* pg. 8.

Bacon, Michael, Male

BAKER, Jams, - He is on the "Petite" Jury list.- *Jury Lists, 1720, Acts #422, [at South Carolina Archives],* pg. 11.

Baker, Jams, Male

BAKER, Jno, Senr, - He is on the "Petite" Jury list.- *Jury Lists, 1720, Acts #422, [at South Carolina Archives],* pg. 8.

Baker, Jno, Senr, Male

BAKER, Richd, - He is on the "Petite" Jury list.- *Jury Lists, 1720, Acts #422, [at South Carolina Archives],* pg. 11.

Baker, Richd, Male

BAKER, Thos, - He is on the "Petite" Jury list.- *Jury Lists, 1720, Acts #422, [at South Carolina Archives],* pg. 8.

Baker, Thos, Male

BALEY, Ralph, - He is on the "Petite" Jury list.- *Jury Lists, 1720, Acts #422, [at South Carolina Archives],* pg. 5.

Baley, Ralph, Male

BALL, Elias, - He is on the Grand Jury list.- *Jury Lists, 1720, Acts #422, [at South Carolina Archives],* pg. 3.

Ball, Elias, Male

BALL, Elias, - He is on the "Petite" Jury list.- *Jury Lists, 1720, Acts #422, [at South Carolina Archives],* pg. 11.

Ball, Elias, Male

BALL, Richd, - He is on the "Petite" Jury list.- *Jury Lists, 1720, Acts #422, [at South Carolina Archives],* pg. 11.

Ball, Richd, Male

BALL, Robt, - He is on the "Petite" Jury list.- *Jury Lists, 1720, Acts #422, [at South Carolina Archives],* pg. 11.

Ball, Robt, Male

BALL, Wm, - He is on the "Petite" Jury list.- *Jury Lists, 1720, Acts #422, [at South Carolina Archives],* pg. 11.

Ball, Wm, Male

BALLENTINE, Jno, - He is on the "Petite" Jury list.- *Jury Lists, 1720, Acts #422, [at South Carolina Archives],* pg. 8.

Ballentine, Jno, Male

BARKSDALE, Thos, - He is on the "Petite" Jury list.- *Jury Lists, 1720, Acts #422, [at South Carolina Archives],* pg. 13.

Barksdale, Thos, Male

BARKSDALE, Thos, - He is on the Grand Jury list.- *Jury Lists, 1720, Acts #422, [at South Carolina Archives],* pg. 3.

Barksdale, Thos, Male

BARLOW, Thos, - He is on the Grand Jury list.- *Jury Lists, 1720, Acts #422, [at South Carolina Archives],* pg. 3.

Barlow, Thos, Male

BARNES, Thos, - He is on the "Petite" Jury list.- *Jury Lists, 1720, Acts #422, [at South Carolina Archives],* pg. 4.

Barnes, Thos, Male

BARRY, Josph, - He is on the "Petite" Jury list.- *Jury Lists, 1720, Acts #422, [at South Carolina Archives],* pg. 9.

Barry, Josph, Male

BARTON, Thos, - He is on the "Petite" Jury list.- *Jury Lists, 1720, Acts #422, [at South Carolina Archives],* pg. 3.

Barton, Thos, Male

BASKERFIELD, Jasper, - He is on the "Petite" Jury list.- *Jury Lists, 1720, Acts #422, [at South Carolina Archives],* pg. 12.

Baskerfield, Jasper, Male

BATCHELOR, Davd, - He is on the "Petite" Jury list.- *Jury Lists, 1720, Acts #422, [at South Carolina Archives],* pg. 11.

Batchelor, Davd, Male

BATTOONE, Isaac, - He is on the "Petite" Jury list.- *Jury Lists, 1720, Acts #422, [at South Carolina Archives],* pg. 6.

Battoone, Isaac, Male

BEAMER, Jno, - He is on the "Petite" Jury list.- *Jury Lists, 1720, Acts #422, [at South Carolina Archives],* pg. 3.

Beamer, Jno, Male

BEAMER, Jno, - He is on the Grand Jury list.- *Jury Lists, 1720, Acts #422, [at South Carolina Archives],* pg. 1.

Beamer, Jno, Male

BEARD, Matthew, - He is on the "Petite" Jury list.- *Jury Lists, 1720, Acts #422, [at South Carolina Archives],* pg. 10.

Beard, Matthew, Male

BEATON, Richd, - He is on the Grand Jury list.-

Jury Lists, 1720, Acts #422, [at South Carolina Archives], pg. 2.
    Beaton, Richd, Male
BEATTON?, Richd, - He is on the "Petite" Jury list.- *Jury Lists, 1720, Acts #422, [at South Carolina Archives]*, pg. 7.
    Beatton?, Richd, Male
BEAUCHAMP, Adam, - He is on the "Petite" Jury list.- *Jury Lists, 1720, Acts #422, [at South Carolina Archives]*, pg. 9.
    Beauchamp, Adam, Male
BEAUCHET, Nichs, - He is on the "Petite" Jury list.- *Jury Lists, 1720, Acts #422, [at South Carolina Archives]*, pg. 11.
    Beauchet, Nichs, Male
BEE, Jno, Capt, - He is on the "Petite" Jury list.- *Jury Lists, 1720, Acts #422, [at South Carolina Archives]*, pg. 4.
    Bee, Jno, Capt, Male
BEE, Jno, Capt, - He is on the Grand Jury list.- *Jury Lists, 1720, Acts #422, [at South Carolina Archives]*, pg. 1.
    Bee, Jno, Capt, Male
BEE, Thos, - He is on the "Petite" Jury list.- *Jury Lists, 1720, Acts #422, [at South Carolina Archives]*, pg. 9.
    Bee, Thos, Male
BEITAN, Stepn, - He is on the "Petite" Jury list.- *Jury Lists, 1720, Acts #422, [at South Carolina Archives]*, pg. 9.
    Beitan, Stepn, Male
BELL, Jno, Junr, - He is on the "Petite" Jury list.- *Jury Lists, 1720, Acts #422, [at South Carolina Archives]*, pg. 13.
    Bell, Jno, Junr, Male
BELL, Jno, Senr, - He is on the "Petite" Jury list.- *Jury Lists, 1720, Acts #422, [at South Carolina Archives]*, pg. 13.
    Bell, Jno, Senr, Male
BELLAMY, Timo, - He is on the "Petite" Jury list.- *Jury Lists, 1720, Acts #422, [at South Carolina Archives]*, pg. 9.
    Bellamy, Timo, Male
BELLIMY, Timo, - He is on the Grand Jury list.- *Jury Lists, 1720, Acts #422, [at South Carolina Archives]*, pg. 2.
    Bellimy, Timo, Male
BELLIN, Jams, - He is on the "Petite" Jury list.- *Jury Lists, 1720, Acts #422, [at South Carolina Archives]*, pg. 12.
    Bellin, Jams, Male

BELLINGER, Edmund, - He is on the "Petite" Jury list.- *Jury Lists, 1720, Acts #422, [at South Carolina Archives]*, pg. 7.
    Bellinger, Edmund, Male
BELLINGER, Edmund, - He is on the Grand Jury list.- *Jury Lists, 1720, Acts #422, [at South Carolina Archives]*, pg. 2.
    Bellinger, Edmund, Male
BENNIT, Jno, - He is on the "Petite" Jury list.- *Jury Lists, 1720, Acts #422, [at South Carolina Archives]*, pg. 13.
    Bennit, Jno, Male
BENSON, Geo, - He is on the Grand Jury list.- *Jury Lists, 1720, Acts #422, [at South Carolina Archives]*, pg. 2.
    Benson, Geo, Male
BENYSON, Geo, - He is on the "Petite" Jury list.- *Jury Lists, 1720, Acts #422, [at South Carolina Archives]*, pg. 13.
    Benyson, Geo, Male
BERESFORD, Richd, - He is on the "Petite" Jury list.- *Jury Lists, 1720, Acts #422, [at South Carolina Archives]*, pg. 12.
    Beresford, Richd, Male
BERESFORD, Richd, - He is on the Grand Jury list.- *Jury Lists, 1720, Acts #422, [at South Carolina Archives]*, pg. 3.
    Beresford, Richd, Male
BETTESON, Jon, - He is on the "Petite" Jury list.- *Jury Lists, 1720, Acts #422, [at South Carolina Archives]*, pg. 4.
    Betteson, Jon, Male
BILBEAU, Jams, - He is on the "Petite" Jury list.- *Jury Lists, 1720, Acts #422, [at South Carolina Archives]*, pg. 11.
    Bilbeau, Jams, Male
BLACKWEL, Michl, - He is on the "Petite" Jury list.- *Jury Lists, 1720, Acts #422, [at South Carolina Archives]*, pg. 11.
    Blackwel, Michl, Male
BLAKE, Jno, - He is on the "Petite" Jury list.- *Jury Lists, 1720, Acts #422, [at South Carolina Archives]*, pg. 10.
    Blake, Jno, Male
BODDETT, Isaac, - He is on the "Petite" Jury list.- *Jury Lists, 1720, Acts #422, [at South Carolina Archives]*, pg. 6.
    Boddett, Isaac, Male
BOIGARD, Mathw, - He is on the "Petite" Jury list.- *Jury Lists, 1720, Acts #422, [at South Carolina Archives]*, pg. 9.

Boigard, Mathw, Male

BOINEAU, Michle, - He is on the "Petite" Jury list.- *Jury Lists, 1720, Acts #422, [at South Carolina Archives]*, pg. 11.

Boineau, Michle, Male

BOLLOUGH, Wm, - He is on the "Petite" Jury list.- *Jury Lists, 1720, Acts #422, [at South Carolina Archives]*, pg. 13.

Bollough, Wm, Male

BOND, Jacb, - He is on the "Petite" Jury list.- *Jury Lists, 1720, Acts #422, [at South Carolina Archives]*, pg. 13.

Bond, Jacb, Male

BONNEAU, Antho, - He is on the Grand Jury list.- *Jury Lists, 1720, Acts #422, [at South Carolina Archives]*, pg. 3.

Bonneau, Antho, Male

BONNEAU, Antho, - He is on the "Petite" Jury list.- *Jury Lists, 1720, Acts #422, [at South Carolina Archives]*, pg. 11.

Bonneau, Antho, Male

BONNEAU, Jacb, - He is on the "Petite" Jury list.- *Jury Lists, 1720, Acts #422, [at South Carolina Archives]*, pg. 11.

Bonneau, Jacb, Male

BONOTE, Jonas, - He is on the "Petite" Jury list.- *Jury Lists, 1720, Acts #422, [at South Carolina Archives]*, pg. 12.

Bonote, Jonas, Male

BOONE, Thos, - He is on the Grand Jury list.- *Jury Lists, 1720, Acts #422, [at South Carolina Archives]*, pg. 3.

Boone, Thos, Male

BOONE, Thos, - He is on the "Petite" Jury list.- *Jury Lists, 1720, Acts #422, [at South Carolina Archives]*, pg. 13.

Boone, Thos, Male

BOSSWARD, Jams, - He is on the "Petite" Jury list.- *Jury Lists, 1720, Acts #422, [at South Carolina Archives]*, pg. 8.

Bossward, Jams, Male

BOWERS, Henry, - He is on the "Petite" Jury list.- *Jury Lists, 1720, Acts #422, [at South Carolina Archives]*, pg. 5.

Bowers, Henry, Male

BRAILSFORD, Edwd, - He is on the Grand Jury list.- *Jury Lists, 1720, Acts #422, [at South Carolina Archives]*, pg. 2.

Brailsford, Edwd, Male

BRAILSFORD, Samle, - He is on the "Petite" Jury list.- *Jury Lists, 1720, Acts #422, [at South Carolina Archives]*, pg. 7.

Brailsford, Samle, Male

BRAISEUR, Fras, - He is on the "Petite" Jury list.- *Jury Lists, 1720, Acts #422, [at South Carolina Archives]*, pg. 9.

Braiseur, Fras, Male

BRANDFORD, Jno, Junr, - He is on the "Petite" Jury list.- *Jury Lists, 1720, Acts #422, [at South Carolina Archives]*, pg. 8.

Brandford, Jno, Junr, Male

BRANFORD, Jno, Senr, - He is on the "Petite" Jury list.- *Jury Lists, 1720, Acts #422, [at South Carolina Archives]*, pg. 8.

Branford, Jno, Senr, Male

BRANFORD, Wm, - He is on the "Petite" Jury list.- *Jury Lists, 1720, Acts #422, [at South Carolina Archives]*, pg. 7.

Branford, Wm, Male

BRANN, Jno, Senr, - He is on the "Petite" Jury list.- *Jury Lists, 1720, Acts #422, [at South Carolina Archives]*, pg. 9.

Brann, Jno, Senr, Male

BRETON, Jno, - He is on the "Petite" Jury list.- *Jury Lists, 1720, Acts #422, [at South Carolina Archives]*, pg. 9.

Breton, Jno, Male

BREWINGTON, Robt, - He is on the "Petite" Jury list.- *Jury Lists, 1720, Acts #422, [at South Carolina Archives]*, pg. 9.

Brewington, Robt, Male

BRIMAR, Jams, - He is on the "Petite" Jury list.- *Jury Lists, 1720, Acts #422, [at South Carolina Archives]*, pg. 11.

Brimar, Jams, Male

BRIMAR, Peter, - He is on the "Petite" Jury list.- *Jury Lists, 1720, Acts #422, [at South Carolina Archives]*, pg. 11.

Brimar, Peter, Male

BRITTON, Frans, Senr, - He is on the "Petite" Jury list.- *Jury Lists, 1720, Acts #422, [at South Carolina Archives]*, pg. 12.

Britton, Frans, Senr, Male

BRITTON, Jno, - He is on the "Petite" Jury list.- *Jury Lists, 1720, Acts #422, [at South Carolina Archives]*, pg. 13.

Britton, Jno, Male

BROCKINGTOWN, Wm, - He is on the "Petite" Jury list.- *Jury Lists, 1720, Acts #422, [at South Carolina Archives]*, pg. 12.

Brockingtown, Wm, Male
BROUGHTON, Andw, - He is on the "Petite"
Jury list.- *Jury Lists, 1720, Acts #422, [at South
Carolina Archives]*, pg. 11.
Broughton, Andw, Male
BROUGHTON, Nathanle, - He is on the Grand
Jury list.- *Jury Lists, 1720, Acts #422, [at South
Carolina Archives]*, pg. 3.
Broughton, Nathanle, Male
BROUGHTON, Nathle, - He is on the "Petite"
Jury list.- *Jury Lists, 1720, Acts #422, [at South
Carolina Archives]*, pg. 11.
Broughton, Nathle, Male
BROUGHTON, Thos, Colo, - He is on the Grand
Jury list.- *Jury Lists, 1720, Acts #422, [at South
Carolina Archives]*, pg. 3.
Broughton, Thos, Colo, Male
BROUGHTON, Thos, Colo, - He is on the
"Petite" Jury list.- *Jury Lists, 1720, Acts #422, [at
South Carolina Archives]*, pg. 11.
Broughton, Thos, Colo, Male
BROWN, Jams, - He is on the "Petite" Jury list.-
*Jury Lists, 1720, Acts #422, [at South Carolina
Archives]*, pg. 12.
Brown, Jams, Male
BROWN, Jno, - He is on the "Petite" Jury list.-
*Jury Lists, 1720, Acts #422, [at South Carolina
Archives]*, pg. 14.
Brown, Jno, Male
BROWN, Jno, Serjt, - He is on the "Petite" Jury
list.- *Jury Lists, 1720, Acts #422, [at South
Carolina Archives]*, pg. 6.
Brown, Jno, Serjt, Male
BRUINTON, Colo, - He is on the "Petite" Jury
list.- *Jury Lists, 1720, Acts #422, [at South
Carolina Archives]*, pg. 9.
Bruinton, Colo, Male
BRUINTON?, Colo, - He is on the Grand Jury
list.- *Jury Lists, 1720, Acts #422, [at South
Carolina Archives]*, pg. 2.
Bruinton?, Colo, Male
BRUNSTON, Abraham, Senr, - He is on the
"Petite" Jury list.- *Jury Lists, 1720, Acts #422, [at
South Carolina Archives]*, pg. 7.
Brunston, Abraham, Senr, Male
BRUNSTON, Isaac, - He is on the "Petite" Jury
list.- *Jury Lists, 1720, Acts #422, [at South
Carolina Archives]*, pg. 8.
Brunston, Isaac, Male

BRUNSTON, Josph, - He is on the "Petite" Jury
list.- *Jury Lists, 1720, Acts #422, [at South
Carolina Archives]*, pg. 8.
Brunston, Josph, Male
BRYAN, Hugh, Senr, - He is on the "Petite" Jury
list.- *Jury Lists, 1720, Acts #422, [at South
Carolina Archives]*, pg. 4.
Bryan, Hugh, Senr, Male
BRYAN, Joseph, - He is on the "Petite" Jury list.-
*Jury Lists, 1720, Acts #422, [at South Carolina
Archives]*, pg. 4.
Bryan, Joseph, Male
BUGG, Jno, - He is on the "Petite" Jury list.- *Jury
Lists, 1720, Acts #422, [at South Carolina
Archives]*, pg. 8.
Bugg, Jno, Male
BULL, Barnaby, - He is on the Grand Jury list.-
*Jury Lists, 1720, Acts #422, [at South Carolina
Archives]*, pg. 1.
Bull, Barnaby, Male
BULL, Barnaby, - He is on the "Petite" Jury list.-
*Jury Lists, 1720, Acts #422, [at South Carolina
Archives]*, pg. 6.
Bull, Barnaby, Male
BULL, Jno, - He is on the "Petite" Jury list.- *Jury
Lists, 1720, Acts #422, [at South Carolina
Archives]*, pg. 6.
Bull, Jno, Male
BULL, Jno, - He is on the Grand Jury list.- *Jury
Lists, 1720, Acts #422, [at South Carolina
Archives]*, pg. 1.
Bull, Jno, Male
BULL, Wm, Colo, - He is on the "Petite" Jury
list.- *Jury Lists, 1720, Acts #422, [at South
Carolina Archives]*, pg. 7.
Bull, Wm, Colo, Male
BULL, Wm, Colo, - He is on the Grand Jury list.-
*Jury Lists, 1720, Acts #422, [at South Carolina
Archives]*, pg. 2.
Bull, Wm, Colo, Male
BULLIN, Jno, - He is on the "Petite" Jury list.-
*Jury Lists, 1720, Acts #422, [at South Carolina
Archives]*, pg. 9.
Bullin, Jno, Male
BULLIN, Thos, - He is on the "Petite" Jury list.-
*Jury Lists, 1720, Acts #422, [at South Carolina
Archives]*, pg. 10.
Bullin, Thos, Male
BULLUCK, Jno, - He is on the "Petite" Jury list.-
*Jury Lists, 1720, Acts #422, [at South Carolina
Archives]*, pg. 8.

Bulluck, Jno, Male

BURLEY, Abraham, - He is on the "Petite" Jury list.- *Jury Lists, 1720, Acts #422, [at South Carolina Archives]*, pg. 7.

Burley, Abraham, Male

BURLEY, Wm, - He is on the "Petite" Jury list.- *Jury Lists, 1720, Acts #422, [at South Carolina Archives]*, pg. 8.

Burley, Wm, Male

BURNHAM, Chas, - He is on the "Petite" Jury list.- *Jury Lists, 1720, Acts #422, [at South Carolina Archives]*, pg. 7.

Burnham, Chas, Male

BURNHAM, Jno, - He is on the "Petite" Jury list.- *Jury Lists, 1720, Acts #422, [at South Carolina Archives]*, pg. 6.

Burnham, Jno, Male

BURT, Jams, - He is on the Grand Jury list.- *Jury Lists, 1720, Acts #422, [at South Carolina Archives]*, pg. 1.

Burt, Jams, Male

BURTON, Thos, - He is on the "Petite" Jury list.- *Jury Lists, 1720, Acts #422, [at South Carolina Archives]*, pg. 12.

Burton, Thos, Male

BURTT, Jams, - He is on the "Petite" Jury list.- *Jury Lists, 1720, Acts #422, [at South Carolina Archives]*, pg. 4.

Burtt, Jams, Male

BUTLER, Shem, - He is on the Grand Jury list.- *Jury Lists, 1720, Acts #422, [at South Carolina Archives]*, pg. 1.

Butler, Shem, Male

BUTTLER, Richd, - He is on the Grand Jury list.- *Jury Lists, 1720, Acts #422, [at South Carolina Archives]*, pg. 2.

Buttler, Richd, Male

BUTTLER, Richd, - He is on the "Petite" Jury list.- *Jury Lists, 1720, Acts #422, [at South Carolina Archives]*, pg. 7.

Buttler, Richd, Male

BUTTLER, Shem, - He is on the "Petite" Jury list.- *Jury Lists, 1720, Acts #422, [at South Carolina Archives]*, pg. 7.

Buttler, Shem, Male

CANNARD, Jno, - He is on the "Petite" Jury list.- *Jury Lists, 1720, Acts #422, [at South Carolina Archives]*, pg. 13.

Cannard, Jno, Male

CANTY, Geo, - He is on the "Petite" Jury list.- *Jury Lists, 1720, Acts #422, [at South Carolina Archives]*, pg. 7.

Canty, Geo, Male

CANTY, Jno, - He is on the Grand Jury list.- *Jury Lists, 1720, Acts #422, [at South Carolina Archives]*, pg. 2.

Canty, Jno, Male

CANTY, Jno, - He is on the "Petite" Jury list.- *Jury Lists, 1720, Acts #422, [at South Carolina Archives]*, pg. 7.

Canty, Jno, Male

CAPERS, Richd, - He is on the Grand Jury list.- *Jury Lists, 1720, Acts #422, [at South Carolina Archives]*, pg. 1.

Capers, Richd, Male

CAPERS, Richd, - He is on the "Petite" Jury list.- *Jury Lists, 1720, Acts #422, [at South Carolina Archives]*, pg. 4.

Capers, Richd, Male

CAPERS, Thos, - He is on the "Petite" Jury list.- *Jury Lists, 1720, Acts #422, [at South Carolina Archives]*, pg. 9.

Capers, Thos, Male

CARMICHAEL, Jno, - He is on the "Petite" Jury list.- *Jury Lists, 1720, Acts #422, [at South Carolina Archives]*, pg. 10.

Carmichael, Jno, Male

CASWELL, Jno, - He is on the "Petite" Jury list.- *Jury Lists, 1720, Acts #422, [at South Carolina Archives]*, pg. 7.

Caswell, Jno, Male

CATER, Wm, - He is on the "Petite" Jury list.- *Jury Lists, 1720, Acts #422, [at South Carolina Archives]*, pg. 8.

Cater, Wm, Male

CATLE, Petr, - He is on the Grand Jury list.- *Jury Lists, 1720, Acts #422, [at South Carolina Archives]*, pg. 2.

Catle, Petr, Male

CATTLE, Petr, - He is on the "Petite" Jury list.- *Jury Lists, 1720, Acts #422, [at South Carolina Archives]*, pg. 7.

Cattle, Petr, Male

CATTLE, Wm, ?, - He is on the Grand Jury list.- *Jury Lists, 1720, Acts #422, [at South Carolina Archives]*, pg. 2.

Cattle, Wm, ?, Male

CATTLE, Wm, ?, - He is on the "Petite" Jury list.- *Jury Lists, 1720, Acts #422, [at South Carolina Archives]*, pg. 7.

Cattle, Wm, ?, Male

CHAMBERLAINE, Job, - He is on the "Petite" Jury list.- *Jury Lists, 1720, Acts #422, [at South Carolina Archives]*, pg. 8.

Chamberlaine, Job, Male

CHAPLIN, Jno, - He is on the "Petite" Jury list.- *Jury Lists, 1720, Acts #422, [at South Carolina Archives]*, pg. 3.

Chaplin, Jno, Male

CHAPMAN, Wm, - He is on the Grand Jury list.- *Jury Lists, 1720, Acts #422, [at South Carolina Archives]*, pg. 1.

Chapman, Wm, Male

CHAPMAN, Wm, - He is on the "Petite" Jury list.- *Jury Lists, 1720, Acts #422, [at South Carolina Archives]*, pg. 6.

Chapman, Wm, Male

CHICKEN, Geo, Colo, - He is on the "Petite" Jury list.- *Jury Lists, 1720, Acts #422, [at South Carolina Archives]*, pg. 10.

Chicken, Geo, Colo, Male

CHICKEN, Geo, Colo, - He is on the Grand Jury list.- *Jury Lists, 1720, Acts #422, [at South Carolina Archives]*, pg. 3.

Chicken, Geo, Colo, Male

CLAPP, Gilson, - He is on the "Petite" Jury list.- *Jury Lists, 1720, Acts #422, [at South Carolina Archives]*, pg. 9.

Clapp, Gilson, Male

CLARAGE, Geo, - He is on the "Petite" Jury list.- *Jury Lists, 1720, Acts #422, [at South Carolina Archives]*, pg. 3.

Clarage, Geo, Male

CLARK, Jeremiah, - He is on the "Petite" Jury list.- *Jury Lists, 1720, Acts #422, [at South Carolina Archives]*, pg. 5.

Clark, Jeremiah, Male

CLARK, Samle, - He is on the "Petite" Jury list.- *Jury Lists, 1720, Acts #422, [at South Carolina Archives]*, pg. 8.

Clark, Samle, Male

CLIFFORD, Thos, - He is on the "Petite" Jury list.- *Jury Lists, 1720, Acts #422, [at South Carolina Archives]*, pg. 9.

Clifford, Thos, Male

CLIJAT, Robt, - He is on the "Petite" Jury list.- *Jury Lists, 1720, Acts #422, [at South Carolina Archives]*, pg. 11.

Clijat, Robt, Male

CLINCH, Alexr, - He is on the "Petite" Jury list.- *Jury Lists, 1720, Acts #422, [at South Carolina Archives]*, pg. 9.

Clinch, Alexr, Male

COARD, Thos, - He is on the "Petite" Jury list.- *Jury Lists, 1720, Acts #422, [at South Carolina Archives]*, pg. 14.

Coard, Thos, Male

COCKFIELD, Jno, - He is on the "Petite" Jury list.- *Jury Lists, 1720, Acts #422, [at South Carolina Archives]*, pg. 7.

Cockfield, Jno, Male

COCKFIELD, Moses, - He is on the "Petite" Jury list.- *Jury Lists, 1720, Acts #422, [at South Carolina Archives]*, pg. 7.

Cockfield, Moses, Male

CODNER, Richd, - He is on the "Petite" Jury list.- *Jury Lists, 1720, Acts #422, [at South Carolina Archives]*, pg. 12.

Codner, Richd, Male

COLE, Robt, - He is on the "Petite" Jury list.- *Jury Lists, 1720, Acts #422, [at South Carolina Archives]*, pg. 4.

Cole, Robt, Male

COLETON, Charles, Capt, - He is on the "Petite" Jury list.- *Jury Lists, 1720, Acts #422, [at South Carolina Archives]*, pg. 10.

Coleton, Charles, Capt, Male

COLETON, Charles, Capt, - He is on the Grand Jury list.- *Jury Lists, 1720, Acts #422, [at South Carolina Archives]*, pg. 3.

Coleton, Charles, Capt, Male

COLETON, Peter, - He is on the Grand Jury list.- *Jury Lists, 1720, Acts #422, [at South Carolina Archives]*, pg. 3.

Coleton, Peter, Male

COLLENS, Andw, - He is on the "Petite" Jury list.- *Jury Lists, 1720, Acts #422, [at South Carolina Archives]*, pg. 13.

Collens, Andw, Male

COLLETON, Jams, - He is on the "Petite" Jury list.- *Jury Lists, 1720, Acts #422, [at South Carolina Archives]*, pg. 10.

Colleton, Jams, Male

COLLETON, Petr, - He is on the "Petite" Jury list.- *Jury Lists, 1720, Acts #422, [at South Carolina Archives]*, pg. 10.

Colleton, Petr, Male

COLLINS, Alexr, - He is on the "Petite" Jury list.- *Jury Lists, 1720, Acts #422, [at South Carolina Archives]*, pg. 13.

Collins, Alexr, Male
COLLINS, Jonah, - He is on the Grand Jury list.- *Jury Lists, 1720, Acts #422, [at South Carolina Archives],* pg. 3.
Collins, Jonah, Male
COLLINS, Jonah, - He is on the "Petite" Jury list.- *Jury Lists, 1720, Acts #422, [at South Carolina Archives],* pg. 13.
Collins, Jonah, Male
COMMANDER, Samle, - He is on the "Petite" Jury list.- *Jury Lists, 1720, Acts #422, [at South Carolina Archives],* pg. 12.
Commander, Samle, Male
COOK, Garrat, - He is on the "Petite" Jury list.- *Jury Lists, 1720, Acts #422, [at South Carolina Archives],* pg. 13.
Cook, Garrat, Male
COOK, Wm, - He is on the "Petite" Jury list.- *Jury Lists, 1720, Acts #422, [at South Carolina Archives],* pg. 13.
Cook, Wm, Male
COOPER, Jno Murril, - He is on the "Petite" Jury list.- *Jury Lists, 1720, Acts #422, [at South Carolina Archives],* pg. 13.
Cooper, Jno Murril, Male
COOPER, Thos, - He is on the "Petite" Jury list.- *Jury Lists, 1720, Acts #422, [at South Carolina Archives],* pg. 11.
Cooper, Thos, Male
COSTELL, Jams, - He is on the "Petite" Jury list.- *Jury Lists, 1720, Acts #422, [at South Carolina Archives],* pg. 7.
Costell, Jams, Male
COSTELL, Jno, Junr, - He is on the "Petite" Jury list.- *Jury Lists, 1720, Acts #422, [at South Carolina Archives],* pg. 7.
Costell, Jno, Junr, Male
COSTELL, Jno, Senr, - He is on the "Petite" Jury list.- *Jury Lists, 1720, Acts #422, [at South Carolina Archives],* pg. 7.
Costell, Jno, Senr, Male
COWEN, Jno, - He is on the "Petite" Jury list.- *Jury Lists, 1720, Acts #422, [at South Carolina Archives],* pg. 5.
Cowen, Jno, Male
COX, Robt, - He is on the "Petite" Jury list.- *Jury Lists, 1720, Acts #422, [at South Carolina Archives],* pg. 4.
Cox, Robt, Male

COX, Thos, - He is on the "Petite" Jury list.- *Jury Lists, 1720, Acts #422, [at South Carolina Archives],* pg. 6.
Cox, Thos, Male
CROFFTS, Jno, - He is on the "Petite" Jury list.- *Jury Lists, 1720, Acts #422, [at South Carolina Archives],* pg. 4.
Croffts, Jno, Male
CROFFTS, Jno, Capt, - He is on the Grand Jury list.- *Jury Lists, 1720, Acts #422, [at South Carolina Archives],* pg. 2.
Croffts, Jno, Capt, Male
DALTON, Jams, - He is on the "Petite" Jury list.- *Jury Lists, 1720, Acts #422, [at South Carolina Archives],* pg. 9.
Dalton, Jams, Male
DALTON, Wm, - He is on the "Petite" Jury list.- *Jury Lists, 1720, Acts #422, [at South Carolina Archives],* pg. 5.
Dalton, Wm, Male
DANSFORD, Josph, - He is on the "Petite" Jury list.- *Jury Lists, 1720, Acts #422, [at South Carolina Archives],* pg. 6.
Dansford, Josph, Male
DARBY, Michael, - He is on the "Petite" Jury list.- *Jury Lists, 1720, Acts #422, [at South Carolina Archives],* pg. 12.
Darby, Michael, Male
DAVIS, Samle, Junr, - He is on the "Petite" Jury list.- *Jury Lists, 1720, Acts #422, [at South Carolina Archives],* pg. 4.
Davis, Samle, Junr, Male
DAVIS, Samle, Senr, - He is on the "Petite" Jury list.- *Jury Lists, 1720, Acts #422, [at South Carolina Archives],* pg. 4.
Davis, Samle, Senr, Male
DE LA CONSELIER, Benja, - He is on the "Petite" Jury list.- *Jury Lists, 1720, Acts #422, [at South Carolina Archives],* pg. 5.
De La Conselier, Benja, Male
DE LA CONSELIER, Benja, - He is on the Grand Jury list.- *Jury Lists, 1720, Acts #422, [at South Carolina Archives],* pg. 2.
De La Conselier, Benja, Male
DE ST JULIAN, Paul, - He is on the "Petite" Jury list.- *Jury Lists, 1720, Acts #422, [at South Carolina Archives],* pg. 10.
De St Julian, Paul, Male
DEBOURDEAUX, Antho, - He is on the "Petite" Jury list.- *Jury Lists, 1720, Acts #422, [at South Carolina Archives],* pg. 11.

Debourdeaux, Antho, Male

DEDCOTT, Jno, Junr, - He is on the "Petite" Jury list.- *Jury Lists, 1720, Acts #422, [at South Carolina Archives]*, pg. 4.

Dedcott, Jno, Junr, Male

DEDCOTT, Jno, Senr, - He is on the "Petite" Jury list.- *Jury Lists, 1720, Acts #422, [at South Carolina Archives]*, pg. 4.

Dedcott, Jno, Senr, Male

DEDCOTT, Jos, - He is on the "Petite" Jury list.- *Jury Lists, 1720, Acts #422, [at South Carolina Archives]*, pg. 5.

Dedcott, Jos, Male

DEER, Jno, - He is on the "Petite" Jury list.- *Jury Lists, 1720, Acts #422, [at South Carolina Archives]*, pg. 4.

Deer, Jno, Male

DENNIS, Benja, - He is on the "Petite" Jury list.- *Jury Lists, 1720, Acts #422, [at South Carolina Archives]*, pg. 9.

Dennis, Benja, Male

DENNIS, Lawrence, Capt, - He is on the "Petite" Jury list.- *Jury Lists, 1720, Acts #422, [at South Carolina Archives]*, pg. 5.

Dennis, Lawrence, Capt, Male

DENNIS, Lawrence, Capt, - He is on the Grand Jury list.- *Jury Lists, 1720, Acts #422, [at South Carolina Archives]*, pg. 1.

Dennis, Lawrence, Capt, Male

DEVALL, Lewis, - He is on the "Petite" Jury list.- *Jury Lists, 1720, Acts #422, [at South Carolina Archives]*, pg. 8.

Devall, Lewis, Male

DEVEAU, Andrew, - He is on the "Petite" Jury list.- *Jury Lists, 1720, Acts #422, [at South Carolina Archives]*, pg. 11.

Deveau, Andrew, Male

DEVEAU, Andw, - He is on the Grand Jury list.- *Jury Lists, 1720, Acts #422, [at South Carolina Archives]*, pg. 3.

Deveau, Andw, Male

DEVOLL, David, - He is on the "Petite" Jury list.- *Jury Lists, 1720, Acts #422, [at South Carolina Archives]*, pg. 9.

DeVoll, David, Male

DEWS, Robt, - He is on the "Petite" Jury list.- *Jury Lists, 1720, Acts #422, [at South Carolina Archives]*, pg. 8.

Dews, Robt, Male

DINGLE, Josph, - He is on the "Petite" Jury list.- *Jury Lists, 1720, Acts #422, [at South Carolina Archives]*, pg. 10.

Dingle, Josph, Male

DISTON, Charles, - He is on the "Petite" Jury list.- *Jury Lists, 1720, Acts #422, [at South Carolina Archives]*, pg. 7.

Diston, Charles, Male

DIX, Arthr, - He is on the "Petite" Jury list.- *Jury Lists, 1720, Acts #422, [at South Carolina Archives]*, pg. 5.

Dix, Arthr, Male

DOBING, Leonard, - He is on the "Petite" Jury list.- *Jury Lists, 1720, Acts #422, [at South Carolina Archives]*, pg. 8.

Dobing, Leonard, Male

DOUSE, Stephen, - He is on the "Petite" Jury list.- *Jury Lists, 1720, Acts #422, [at South Carolina Archives]*, pg. 8.

Douse, Stephen, Male

DOUXSAINT, Paul, - He is on the "Petite" Jury list.- *Jury Lists, 1720, Acts #422, [at South Carolina Archives]*, pg. 9.

Douxsaint, Paul, Male

DRY, Wm, - He is on the "Petite" Jury list.- *Jury Lists, 1720, Acts #422, [at South Carolina Archives]*, pg. 10.

Dry, Wm, Male

DRY, Wm, - He is on the Grand Jury list.- *Jury Lists, 1720, Acts #422, [at South Carolina Archives]*, pg. 2.

Dry, Wm, Male

DUBOUS, Isaac, - He is on the "Petite" Jury list.- *Jury Lists, 1720, Acts #422, [at South Carolina Archives]*, pg. 13.

Dubous, Isaac, Male

DUBURDU, Samle, - He is on the "Petite" Jury list.- *Jury Lists, 1720, Acts #422, [at South Carolina Archives]*, pg. 10.

Duburdu, Samle, Male

DUCHETT, Geo, - He is on the "Petite" Jury list.- *Jury Lists, 1720, Acts #422, [at South Carolina Archives]*, pg. 8.

Duchett, Geo, Male

DUIZEN, Jno, - He is on the "Petite" Jury list.- *Jury Lists, 1720, Acts #422, [at South Carolina Archives]*, pg. 10.

Duizen, Jno, Male

DUNHAM, Jno, - He is on the "Petite" Jury list.- *Jury Lists, 1720, Acts #422, [at South Carolina Archives]*, pg. 12.

Dunham, Jno, Male

DUPREE, Corns, - He is on the "Petite" Jury list.- *Jury Lists, 1720, Acts #422, [at South Carolina Archives]*, pg. 11.

Dupree, Corns, Male

DUPREE, Josias, - He is on the Grand Jury list.- *Jury Lists, 1720, Acts #422, [at South Carolina Archives]*, pg. 3.

Dupree, Josias, Male

DUPREE, Josias, - He is on the "Petite" Jury list.- *Jury Lists, 1720, Acts #422, [at South Carolina Archives]*, pg. 11.

Dupree, Josias, Male

DURANT, Henry, - He is on the "Petite" Jury list.- *Jury Lists, 1720, Acts #422, [at South Carolina Archives]*, pg. 12.

Durant, Henry, Male

DYMES, Thos, - He is on the "Petite" Jury list.- *Jury Lists, 1720, Acts #422, [at South Carolina Archives]*, pg. 9.

Dymes, Thos, Male

DYMES, Thos, - He is on the Grand Jury list.- *Jury Lists, 1720, Acts #422, [at South Carolina Archives]*, pg. 2.

Dymes, Thos, Male

EDDINGS, Wm, - He is on the "Petite" Jury list.- *Jury Lists, 1720, Acts #422, [at South Carolina Archives]*, pg. 5.

Eddings, Wm, Male

EDWARDS, Jno, - He is on the "Petite" Jury list.- *Jury Lists, 1720, Acts #422, [at South Carolina Archives]*, pg. 5.

Edwards, Jno, Male

EDWARDS, Uriah, - He is on the "Petite" Jury list.- *Jury Lists, 1720, Acts #422, [at South Carolina Archives]*, pg. 8.

Edwards, Uriah, Male

ELDERS, Jno, - He is on the "Petite" Jury list.- *Jury Lists, 1720, Acts #422, [at South Carolina Archives]*, pg. 9.

Elders, Jno, Male

ELLIOT, Thos, Senr, - He is on the "Petite" Jury list.- *Jury Lists, 1720, Acts #422, [at South Carolina Archives]*, pg. 4.

Elliot, Thos, Senr, Male

ELLIOTE, Robt, - He is on the "Petite" Jury list.- *Jury Lists, 1720, Acts #422, [at South Carolina Archives]*, pg. 6.

Elliote, Robt, Male

ELLIOTE, Wm, - He is on the Grand Jury list.- *Jury Lists, 1720, Acts #422, [at South Carolina Archives]*, pg. 1.

Elliote, Wm, Male

ELLIOTE, Wm, Junr, - He is on the "Petite" Jury list.- *Jury Lists, 1720, Acts #422, [at South Carolina Archives]*, pg. 7.

Elliote, Wm, Junr, Male

ELLIOTT, Thos, Senr, - He is on the Grand Jury list.- *Jury Lists, 1720, Acts #422, [at South Carolina Archives]*, pg. 1.

Elliott, Thos, Senr, Male

ELLIS, Edwd, - He is on the "Petite" Jury list.- *Jury Lists, 1720, Acts #422, [at South Carolina Archives]*, pg. 5.

Ellis, Edwd, Male

ELLIS, Thos, - He is on the "Petite" Jury list.- *Jury Lists, 1720, Acts #422, [at South Carolina Archives]*, pg. 6.

Ellis, Thos, Male

ELMES, Ralph, - He is on the Grand Jury list.- *Jury Lists, 1720, Acts #422, [at South Carolina Archives]*, pg. 1.

Elmes, Ralph, Male

ELMES, Ralph, - He is on the "Petite" Jury list.- *Jury Lists, 1720, Acts #422, [at South Carolina Archives]*, pg. 4.

Elmes, Ralph, Male

ELMES, Thos, - He is on the "Petite" Jury list.- *Jury Lists, 1720, Acts #422, [at South Carolina Archives]*, pg. 8.

Elmes, Thos, Male

EVANS, Jonathan, - He is on the "Petite" Jury list.- *Jury Lists, 1720, Acts #422, [at South Carolina Archives]*, pg. 6.

Evans, Jonathan, Male

EVANS, Rowland, - He is on the "Petite" Jury list.- *Jury Lists, 1720, Acts #422, [at South Carolina Archives]*, pg. 6.

Evans, Rowland, Male

EVELEIGH, Samle, Esqr, - He is on the Grand Jury list.- *Jury Lists, 1720, Acts #422, [at South Carolina Archives]*, pg. 2.

Eveleigh, Samle, Esqr, Male

EVELEIGH, Samle, Esqr, - He is on the "Petite" Jury list.- *Jury Lists, 1720, Acts #422, [at South Carolina Archives]*, pg. 9.

Eveleigh, Samle, Esqr, Male

EVENS, Jno, - He is on the "Petite" Jury list.- *Jury Lists, 1720, Acts #422, [at South Carolina Archives]*, pg. 12.

Evens, Jno, Male

EVENS, Jno, - He is on the "Petite" Jury list.- *Jury Lists, 1720, Acts #422, [at South Carolina Archives]*, pg. 13.

Evens, Jno, Male

EVENS, Jona, - He is on the "Petite" Jury list.- *Jury Lists, 1720, Acts #422, [at South Carolina Archives]*, pg. 12.

Evens, Jona, Male

EVERSON, Wm, - He is on the "Petite" Jury list.- *Jury Lists, 1720, Acts #422, [at South Carolina Archives]*, pg. 5.

Everson, Wm, Male

EVES, Abraham, Colo, - He is on the "Petite" Jury list.- *Jury Lists, 1720, Acts #422, [at South Carolina Archives]*, pg. 5.

Eves, Abraham, Colo, Male

EVES, Abrm, Colo, - He is on the Grand Jury list.- *Jury Lists, 1720, Acts #422, [at South Carolina Archives]*, pg. 1.

Eves, Abrm, Colo, Male

EVINS, Randoll, - He is on the "Petite" Jury list.- *Jury Lists, 1720, Acts #422, [at South Carolina Archives]*, pg. 5.

Evins, Randoll, Male

EVINS, Samle, - He is on the "Petite" Jury list.- *Jury Lists, 1720, Acts #422, [at South Carolina Archives]*, pg. 4.

Evins, Samle, Male

FARLEY, Geo, - He is on the "Petite" Jury list.- *Jury Lists, 1720, Acts #422, [at South Carolina Archives]*, pg. 5.

Farley, Geo, Male

FARR, Thos, - He is on the Grand Jury list.- *Jury Lists, 1720, Acts #422, [at South Carolina Archives]*, pg. 1.

Farr, Thos, Male

FARR, Thos, - He is on the "Petite" Jury list.- *Jury Lists, 1720, Acts #422, [at South Carolina Archives]*, pg. 3.

Farr, Thos, Male

FARRIS, Christopher, - He is on the "Petite" Jury list.- *Jury Lists, 1720, Acts #422, [at South Carolina Archives]*, pg. 11.

Farris, Christopher, Male

FARWELL, Henry, - He is on the "Petite" Jury list.- *Jury Lists, 1720, Acts #422, [at South Carolina Archives]*, pg. 11.

Farwell, Henry, Male

FENDALE, Henry, Junr, - He is on the "Petite" Jury list.- *Jury Lists, 1720, Acts #422, [at South Carolina Archives]*, pg. 6.

Fendale, Henry, Junr, Male

FENWICKE, Jno, Colo, - He is on the "Petite" Jury list.- *Jury Lists, 1720, Acts #422, [at South Carolina Archives]*, pg. 6.

Fenwicke, Jno, Colo, Male

FENWICKE, Jno, Colo, - He is on the Grand Jury list.- *Jury Lists, 1720, Acts #422, [at South Carolina Archives]*, pg. 1.

Fenwicke, Jno, Colo, Male

FENWICKE, Robt, Capt, - He is on the "Petite" Jury list.- *Jury Lists, 1720, Acts #422, [at South Carolina Archives]*, pg. 12.

Fenwicke, Robt, Capt, Male

FENWICKE, Robt, Capt, - He is on the Grand Jury list.- *Jury Lists, 1720, Acts #422, [at South Carolina Archives]*, pg. 3.

Fenwicke, Robt Capt, Male

FERGUSON, Davd, - He is on the "Petite" Jury list.- *Jury Lists, 1720, Acts #422, [at South Carolina Archives]*, pg. 7.

Ferguson, Davd, Male

FIELD, Jno, - He is on the "Petite" Jury list.- *Jury Lists, 1720, Acts #422, [at South Carolina Archives]*, pg. 5.

Field, Jno, Male

FISHBURNE, Wm, - He is on the "Petite" Jury list.- *Jury Lists, 1720, Acts #422, [at South Carolina Archives]*, pg. 8.

Fishburne, Wm, Male

FISHREAU, Gideon, - He is on the "Petite" Jury list.- *Jury Lists, 1720, Acts #422, [at South Carolina Archives]*, pg. 10.

Fishreau, Gideon, Male

FITCH, Jona, - He is on the "Petite" Jury list.- *Jury Lists, 1720, Acts #422, [at South Carolina Archives]*, pg. 14.

Fitch, Jona, Male

FITCH, Tobias, Capt, - He is on the "Petite" Jury list.- *Jury Lists, 1720, Acts #422, [at South Carolina Archives]*, pg. 6.

Fitch, Tobias, Capt, Male

FITZGERALD, Jams, - He is on the "Petite" Jury list.- *Jury Lists, 1720, Acts #422, [at South Carolina Archives]*, pg. 12.

FitzGerald, Jams, Male

FLOYD, Richd, - He is on the "Petite" Jury list.- *Jury Lists, 1720, Acts #422, [at South Carolina Archives]*, pg. 4.

Floyd, Richd, Male

FOARD, Geo, - He is on the "Petite" Jury list.- *Jury Lists, 1720, Acts #422, [at South Carolina Archives]*, pg. 4.

Foard, Geo, Male

FOARD, Stephen, Junr, - He is on the "Petite" Jury list.- *Jury Lists, 1720, Acts #422, [at South Carolina Archives]*, pg. 4.

Foard, Stephen, Junr, Male

FOARD, Stephen, Senr, - He is on the "Petite" Jury list.- *Jury Lists, 1720, Acts #422, [at South Carolina Archives]*, pg. 4.

Foard, Stephen, Senr, Male

FOBBY, Jno, - He is on the "Petite" Jury list.- *Jury Lists, 1720, Acts #422, [at South Carolina Archives]*, pg. 5.

Fobby, Jno, Male

FOGARTY, Stephen, - He is on the "Petite" Jury list.- *Jury Lists, 1720, Acts #422, [at South Carolina Archives]*, pg. 12.

Fogarty, Stephen, Male

FOSTER, Arthr, - He is on the "Petite" Jury list.- *Jury Lists, 1720, Acts #422, [at South Carolina Archives]*, pg. 7.

Foster, Arthr, Male

FRAMPTON, Jno, - He is on the "Petite" Jury list.- *Jury Lists, 1720, Acts #422, [at South Carolina Archives]*, pg. 5.

Frampton, Jno, Male

FRAPIER, Paul, - He is on the "Petite" Jury list.- *Jury Lists, 1720, Acts #422, [at South Carolina Archives]*, pg. 10.

Frapier, Paul, Male

FRASIER, Jno, - He is on the "Petite" Jury list.- *Jury Lists, 1720, Acts #422, [at South Carolina Archives]*, pg. 8.

Frasier, Jno, Male

FRIDLING, Danle, - He is on the "Petite" Jury list.- *Jury Lists, 1720, Acts #422, [at South Carolina Archives]*, pg. 8.

Fridling, Danle, Male

FRITH, Samle, - He is on the Grand Jury list.- *Jury Lists, 1720, Acts #422, [at South Carolina Archives]*, pg. 1.

Frith, Samle, Male

FRITH?, Samle, - He is on the "Petite" Jury list.- *Jury Lists, 1720, Acts #422, [at South Carolina Archives]*, pg. 6.

Frith?, Samle, Male

FULLER, Richd, - He is on the "Petite" Jury list.- *Jury Lists, 1720, Acts #422, [at South Carolina Archives]*, pg. 8.

Fuller, Richd, Male

FULLER, Wm, Senr, - He is on the "Petite" Jury list.- *Jury Lists, 1720, Acts #422, [at South Carolina Archives]*, pg. 8.

Fuller, Wm, Senr, Male

FURBUSH, Wm, - He is on the "Petite" Jury list.- *Jury Lists, 1720, Acts #422, [at South Carolina Archives]*, pg. 13.

Furbush, Wm, Male

FURBUSH, Wm, - He is on the Grand Jury list.- *Jury Lists, 1720, Acts #422, [at South Carolina Archives]*, pg. 3.

Furbush, Wm, Male

GADSDEN, - He is on the "Petite" Jury list.- *Jury Lists, 1720, Acts #422, [at South Carolina Archives]*, pg. 7.

Gadsden, Male

GALE, Danle, - He is on the "Petite" Jury list.- *Jury Lists, 1720, Acts #422, [at South Carolina Archives]*, pg. 14.

Gale, Danle, Male

GANDRON, Jno, Capt, - He is on the Grand Jury list.- *Jury Lists, 1720, Acts #422, [at South Carolina Archives]*, pg. 2.

Gandron, Jno, Capt, Male

GANDRON, Jno, Capt, - He is on the "Petite" Jury list.- *Jury Lists, 1720, Acts #422, [at South Carolina Archives]*, pg. 9.

Gandron, Jno, Capt, Male

GANTLETT, Jno, - He is on the "Petite" Jury list.- *Jury Lists, 1720, Acts #422, [at South Carolina Archives]*, pg. 6.

Gantlett, Jno, Male

GARRAT, Petr, - He is on the "Petite" Jury list.- *Jury Lists, 1720, Acts #422, [at South Carolina Archives]*, pg. 14.

Garrat, Petr, Male

GIBBES, Benja, - He is on the "Petite" Jury list.- *Jury Lists, 1720, Acts #422, [at South Carolina Archives]*, pg. 10.

Gibbes, Benja, Male

GIBBES, Benja, - He is on the Grand Jury list.- *Jury Lists, 1720, Acts #422, [at South Carolina Archives]*, pg. 2.

Gibbes, Benja, Male

GIBBES, Jno, - He is on the Grand Jury list.- *Jury Lists, 1720, Acts #422, [at South Carolina Archives]*, pg. 2.

Gibbes, Jno, Male

GIBBES, John, ?, - He is on the "Petite" Jury list.- *Jury Lists, 1720, Acts #422, [at South Carolina Archives]*, pg. 5.

Gibbes, John, ?, Male

GIBBES, Wm, - He is on the Grand Jury list.- *Jury Lists, 1720, Acts #422, [at South Carolina Archives]*, pg. 2.

Gibbes, Wm, Male

GIBBES, Wm, - He is on the "Petite" Jury list.- *Jury Lists, 1720, Acts #422, [at South Carolina Archives]*, pg. 7.

Gibbes, Wm, Male

GIBBON, Wm, - He is on the "Petite" Jury list.- *Jury Lists, 1720, Acts #422, [at South Carolina Archives]*, pg. 9.

Gibbon, Wm, Male

GIBBON, Wm, - He is on the Grand Jury list.- *Jury Lists, 1720, Acts #422, [at South Carolina Archives]*, pg. 2.

Gibbon, Wm, Male

GIBBONS, Thos, - He is on the "Petite" Jury list.- *Jury Lists, 1720, Acts #422, [at South Carolina Archives]*, pg. 6.

Gibbons, Thos, Male

GIBBS, Jno, ?, - He is on the Grand Jury list.- *Jury Lists, 1720, Acts #422, [at South Carolina Archives]*, pg. 1.

Gibbs, Jno, ?, Male

GIGNILACK, Henry, - He is on the "Petite" Jury list.- *Jury Lists, 1720, Acts #422, [at South Carolina Archives]*, pg. 9.

Gignilack, Henry, Male

GILBERSON, James, - He is on the "Petite" Jury list.- *Jury Lists, 1720, Acts #422, [at South Carolina Archives]*, pg. 3.

Gilberson, James, Male

GILBERSON, Jams, - He is on the Grand Jury list.- *Jury Lists, 1720, Acts #422, [at South Carolina Archives]*, pg. 1.

Gilberson, Jams, Male

GILL, Henry, Junr, - He is on the "Petite" Jury list.- *Jury Lists, 1720, Acts #422, [at South Carolina Archives]*, pg. 12.

Gill, Henry, Junr, Male

GILL, Henry, Senr, - He is on the "Petite" Jury list.- *Jury Lists, 1720, Acts #422, [at South Carolina Archives]*, pg. 12.

Gill, Henry, Senr, Male

GILL, Jams, - He is on the "Petite" Jury list.- *Jury Lists, 1720, Acts #422, [at South Carolina Archives]*, pg. 12.

Gill, Jams, Male

GLAZE, Malachia, - He is on the Grand Jury list.- *Jury Lists, 1720, Acts #422, [at South Carolina Archives]*, pg. 2.

Glaze, Malachia, Male

GLAZE, Malachia, - He is on the "Petite" Jury list.- *Jury Lists, 1720, Acts #422, [at South Carolina Archives]*, pg. 7.

Glaze, Malachia, Male

GODEN, Benja, - He is on the Grand Jury list.- *Jury Lists, 1720, Acts #422, [at South Carolina Archives]*, pg. 3.

Goden, Benja, Male

GODEN, Benja, - He is on the "Petite" Jury list.- *Jury Lists, 1720, Acts #422, [at South Carolina Archives]*, pg. 10.

Goden, Benja, Male

GODFREY, Richd, Lieut, - He is on the Grand Jury list.- *Jury Lists, 1720, Acts #422, [at South Carolina Archives]*, pg. 1.

Godfrey, Richd, Lieut, Male

GODFREY, Richd, Lieut, - He is on the "Petite" Jury list.- *Jury Lists, 1720, Acts #422, [at South Carolina Archives]*, pg. 6.

Godfrey, Richd, Lieut, Male

GODFREY, Robt, - He is on the "Petite" Jury list.- *Jury Lists, 1720, Acts #422, [at South Carolina Archives]*, pg. 3.

Godfrey, Robt, Male

GODFRY, Jno, Capt, - He is on the "Petite" Jury list.- *Jury Lists, 1720, Acts #422, [at South Carolina Archives]*, pg. 7.

Godfry, Jno, Capt, Male

GODFRY, Jno, Capt, - He is on the Grand Jury list.- *Jury Lists, 1720, Acts #422, [at South Carolina Archives]*, pg. 2.

Godfry, Jno, Capt, Male

GOFEL ALIAS MOORE, Jno, - He is on the Grand Jury list.- *Jury Lists, 1720, Acts #422, [at South Carolina Archives]*, pg. 3.

Gofel alias Moore, Jno, Male

GOLDING, Petr, - He is on the "Petite" Jury list.- *Jury Lists, 1720, Acts #422, [at South Carolina Archives]*, pg. 8.

Golding, Petr, Male

GOODBE, Alexr, - He is on the "Petite" Jury list.- *Jury Lists, 1720, Acts #422, [at South Carolina Archives]*, pg. 10.

Goodbe, Alexr, Male
GOODBE, Jams, - He is on the "Petite" Jury list.- *Jury Lists, 1720, Acts #422, [at South Carolina Archives]*, pg. 10.
Goodbe, Jams, Male
GOODBE, Jno, Junr, - He is on the "Petite" Jury list.- *Jury Lists, 1720, Acts #422, [at South Carolina Archives]*, pg. 10.
Goodbe, Jno, Junr, Male
GOODBE, Josph, - He is on the "Petite" Jury list.- *Jury Lists, 1720, Acts #422, [at South Carolina Archives]*, pg. 10.
Goodbe, Josph, Male
GORING, Thos, Senr, - He is on the "Petite" Jury list.- *Jury Lists, 1720, Acts #422, [at South Carolina Archives]*, pg. 8.
Goring, Thos, Senr, Male
GREEN, Danle, - He is on the "Petite" Jury list.- *Jury Lists, 1720, Acts #422, [at South Carolina Archives]*, pg. 4.
Green, Danle, Male
GREEN, Danle, - He is on the Grand Jury list.- *Jury Lists, 1720, Acts #422, [at South Carolina Archives]*, pg. 1.
Green, Danle, Male
GREEN, Jams, Junr, - He is on the "Petite" Jury list.- *Jury Lists, 1720, Acts #422, [at South Carolina Archives]*, pg. 4.
Green, Jams, Junr, Male
GREEN, Jno, - He is on the "Petite" Jury list.- *Jury Lists, 1720, Acts #422, [at South Carolina Archives]*, pg. 6.
Green, Jno, Male
GREEN, Jno, - He is on the "Petite" Jury list.- *Jury Lists, 1720, Acts #422, [at South Carolina Archives]*, pg. 9.
Green, Jno, Male
GREEN, Joshua, - He is on the "Petite" Jury list.- *Jury Lists, 1720, Acts #422, [at South Carolina Archives]*, pg. 10.
Green, Joshua, Male
GREENLAND, Jno, - He is on the "Petite" Jury list.- *Jury Lists, 1720, Acts #422, [at South Carolina Archives]*, pg. 14.
Greenland, Jno, Male
GREENLAND, Wm, - He is on the "Petite" Jury list.- *Jury Lists, 1720, Acts #422, [at South Carolina Archives]*, pg. 11.
Greenland, Wm, Male

GRIFFEN, Joseph, Senr, - He is on the "Petite" Jury list.- *Jury Lists, 1720, Acts #422, [at South Carolina Archives]*, pg. 8.
Griffen, Joseph, Senr, Male
GRIMBOL, Thos, - He is on the "Petite" Jury list.- *Jury Lists, 1720, Acts #422, [at South Carolina Archives]*, pg. 5.
Grimbol, Thos, Male
GUERIN, Vincent, - He is on the "Petite" Jury list.- *Jury Lists, 1720, Acts #422, [at South Carolina Archives]*, pg. 12.
Guerin, Vincent, Male
GUERRING, Petr, - He is on the "Petite" Jury list.- *Jury Lists, 1720, Acts #422, [at South Carolina Archives]*, pg. 10.
Guerring, Petr, Male
GUERY, Peter, - He is on the "Petite" Jury list.- *Jury Lists, 1720, Acts #422, [at South Carolina Archives]*, pg. 13.
Guery, Peter, Male
GUPHEL ALIAS MOORE, Jno, - He is on the "Petite" Jury list.- *Jury Lists, 1720, Acts #422, [at South Carolina Archives]*, pg. 11.
Guphel Alias Moore, Jno, Male
GWIN, Jno, - He is on the "Petite" Jury list.- *Jury Lists, 1720, Acts #422, [at South Carolina Archives]*, pg. 4.
Gwin, Jno, Male
HAILES, Jno, - He is on the "Petite" Jury list.- *Jury Lists, 1720, Acts #422, [at South Carolina Archives]*, pg. 13.
Hailes, Jno, Male
HALE, Arthr, Majr, - He is on the "Petite" Jury list.- *Jury Lists, 1720, Acts #422, [at South Carolina Archives]*, pg. 5.
Hale, Arthr, Majr, Male
HALL, Arthur, Majr, - He is on the Grand Jury list.- *Jury Lists, 1720, Acts #422, [at South Carolina Archives]*, pg. 1.
Hall, Arthur, Majr, Male
HALL, Richd, - He is on the "Petite" Jury list.- *Jury Lists, 1720, Acts #422, [at South Carolina Archives]*, pg. 13.
Hall, Richd, Male
HAMBLING, Thos, - He is on the "Petite" Jury list.- *Jury Lists, 1720, Acts #422, [at South Carolina Archives]*, pg. 13.
Hambling, Thos, Male
HAMELTON, Jno, - He is on the "Petite" Jury list.- *Jury Lists, 1720, Acts #422, [at South Carolina Archives]*, pg. 5.

Hamelton, Jno, Male

HAMELTON, Paul, - He is on the "Petite" Jury list.- *Jury Lists, 1720, Acts #422, [at South Carolina Archives],* pg. 5.

Hamelton, Paul, Male

HAMELTON, Paul, - He is on the Grand Jury list.- *Jury Lists, 1720, Acts #422, [at South Carolina Archives],* pg. 1.

Hamelton, Paul, Male

HANCOCK, Elias, - He is on the "Petite" Jury list.- *Jury Lists, 1720, Acts #422, [at South Carolina Archives],* pg. 9.

Hancock, Elias, Male

HARBIN, Richd, - He is on the "Petite" Jury list.- *Jury Lists, 1720, Acts #422, [at South Carolina Archives],* pg. 10.

Harbin, Richd, Male

HARBUT, Thos, - He is on the "Petite" Jury list.- *Jury Lists, 1720, Acts #422, [at South Carolina Archives],* pg. 13.

Harbut, Thos, Male

HARLESON, Jno, - He is on the Grand Jury list.- *Jury Lists, 1720, Acts #422, [at South Carolina Archives],* pg. 3.

Harleson, Jno, Male

HARLESTON, John, - He is on the "Petite" Jury list.- *Jury Lists, 1720, Acts #422, [at South Carolina Archives],* pg. 11.

Harleston, John, Male

HARRIS, Richd, Capt, - He is on the "Petite" Jury list.- *Jury Lists, 1720, Acts #422, [at South Carolina Archives],* pg. 11.

Harris, Richd, Capt, Male

HARRIS, Richd, Capt, - He is on the Grand Jury list.- *Jury Lists, 1720, Acts #422, [at South Carolina Archives],* pg. 3.

Harris, Richd, Capt, Male

HARVEY, Morris, - He is on the "Petite" Jury list.- *Jury Lists, 1720, Acts #422, [at South Carolina Archives],* pg. 8.

Harvey, Morris, Male

HATCHER, Nicholas, - He is on the "Petite" Jury list.- *Jury Lists, 1720, Acts #422, [at South Carolina Archives],* pg. 5.

Hatcher, Nicholas, Male

HAWKS, Jno, - He is on the "Petite" Jury list.- *Jury Lists, 1720, Acts #422, [at South Carolina Archives],* pg. 8.

Hawks, Jno, Male

HAYES, Chas, - He is on the Grand Jury list.- *Jury Lists, 1720, Acts #422, [at South Carolina Archives],* pg. 3.

Hayes, Chas, Male

HAYES, Chas, - He is on the "Petite" Jury list.- *Jury Lists, 1720, Acts #422, [at South Carolina Archives],* pg. 11.

Hayes, Chas, Male

HAYES, Jno, - He is on the Grand Jury list.- *Jury Lists, 1720, Acts #422, [at South Carolina Archives],* pg. 3.

Hayes, Jno, Male

HAYNES, Robt, - He is on the "Petite" Jury list.- *Jury Lists, 1720, Acts #422, [at South Carolina Archives],* pg. 9.

Haynes, Robt, Male

HAYS, Jno, - He is on the "Petite" Jury list.- *Jury Lists, 1720, Acts #422, [at South Carolina Archives],* pg. 13.

Hays, Jno, Male

HAZARD, Wm, - He is on the "Petite" Jury list.- *Jury Lists, 1720, Acts #422, [at South Carolina Archives],* pg. 5.

Hazard, Wm, Male

HEAPE, Josph, - He is on the "Petite" Jury list.- *Jury Lists, 1720, Acts #422, [at South Carolina Archives],* pg. 6.

Heape, Josph, Male

HEARNE, Jno, - He is on the Grand Jury list.- *Jury Lists, 1720, Acts #422, [at South Carolina Archives],* pg. 1.

Hearne, Jno, Male

HEARNE, Jno, - He is on the "Petite" Jury list.- *Jury Lists, 1720, Acts #422, [at South Carolina Archives],* pg. 6.

Hearne, Jno, Male

HENDRAKES, Jno, - He is on the "Petite" Jury list.- *Jury Lists, 1720, Acts #422, [at South Carolina Archives],* pg. 12.

Hendrakes, Jno, Male

HENDRICK, Danle, - He is on the "Petite" Jury list.- *Jury Lists, 1720, Acts #422, [at South Carolina Archives],* pg. 4.

Hendrick, Danle, Male

HENDRICK, Wm, - He is on the "Petite" Jury list.- *Jury Lists, 1720, Acts #422, [at South Carolina Archives],* pg. 4.

Hendrick, Wm, Male

HENDRICKS, Timo, - He is on the "Petite" Jury list.- *Jury Lists, 1720, Acts #422, [at South Carolina Archives],* pg. 5.

Hendricks, Timo, Male

HERBERT, Jno, - He is on the "Petite" Jury list.- *Jury Lists, 1720, Acts #422, [at South Carolina Archives]*, pg. 10.

Herbert, Jno, Male

HERBERT, Jno, - He is on the Grand Jury list.- *Jury Lists, 1720, Acts #422, [at South Carolina Archives]*, pg. 2.

Herbert, Jno, Male

HEXT, Alexn, Capt, - He is on the Grand Jury list.- *Jury Lists, 1720, Acts #422, [at South Carolina Archives]*, pg. 1.

Hext, Alexn, Capt, Male

HEXT, Alexr, Capt, - He is on the "Petite" Jury list.- *Jury Lists, 1720, Acts #422, [at South Carolina Archives]*, pg. 3.

Hext, Alexr, Capt, Male

HEXT, Annias, - He is on the "Petite" Jury list.- *Jury Lists, 1720, Acts #422, [at South Carolina Archives]*, pg. 3.

Hext, Annias, Male

HEXT, Davd, - He is on the "Petite" Jury list.- *Jury Lists, 1720, Acts #422, [at South Carolina Archives]*, pg. 3.

Hext, Davd, Male

HEXT, Fras, Ensigne, - He is on the "Petite" Jury list.- *Jury Lists, 1720, Acts #422, [at South Carolina Archives]*, pg. 3.

Hext, Fras, Ensigne, Male

HEXT, Hugh, - He is on the "Petite" Jury list.- *Jury Lists, 1720, Acts #422, [at South Carolina Archives]*, pg. 3.

Hext, Hugh, Male

HEXT, Hugh, - He is on the Grand Jury list.- *Jury Lists, 1720, Acts #422, [at South Carolina Archives]*, pg. 1.

Hext, Hugh, Male

HILL, Chas, ?, - He is on the Grand Jury list.- *Jury Lists, 1720, Acts #422, [at South Carolina Archives]*, pg. 2.

Hill, Chas, ?, Male

HILL, Chas, Esqr, - He is on the "Petite" Jury list.- *Jury Lists, 1720, Acts #422, [at South Carolina Archives]*, pg. 9.

Hill, Chas, Esqr, Male

HILL, Jno, - He is on the "Petite" Jury list.- *Jury Lists, 1720, Acts #422, [at South Carolina Archives]*, pg. 4.

Hill, Jno, Male

HILL, Josph, - He is on the "Petite" Jury list.- *Jury Lists, 1720, Acts #422, [at South Carolina Archives]*, pg. 6.

Hill, Josph, Male

HILL, Thos, - He is on the "Petite" Jury list.- *Jury Lists, 1720, Acts #422, [at South Carolina Archives]*, pg. 7.

Hill, Thos, Male

HILL, Wm, - He is on the "Petite" Jury list.- *Jury Lists, 1720, Acts #422, [at South Carolina Archives]*, pg. 6.

Hill, Wm, Male

HISKETT, Geo, - He is on the "Petite" Jury list.- *Jury Lists, 1720, Acts #422, [at South Carolina Archives]*, pg. 9.

Hiskett, Geo, Male

HOGSDON, Jno, - He is on the "Petite" Jury list.- *Jury Lists, 1720, Acts #422, [at South Carolina Archives]*, pg. 9.

Hogsdon, Jno, Male

HOLLY, Josph, - He is on the "Petite" Jury list.- *Jury Lists, 1720, Acts #422, [at South Carolina Archives]*, pg. 5.

Holly, Josph, Male

HOLMAN, Thos, - He is on the "Petite" Jury list.- *Jury Lists, 1720, Acts #422, [at South Carolina Archives]*, pg. 6.

Holman, Thos, Male

HOLMES, Frans, - He is on the Grand Jury list.- *Jury Lists, 1720, Acts #422, [at South Carolina Archives]*, pg. 2.

Holmes, Frans, Male

HOLMES, Fras, - He is on the "Petite" Jury list.- *Jury Lists, 1720, Acts #422, [at South Carolina Archives]*, pg. 8.

Holmes, Fras, Male

HOLMES, Wm, - He is on the "Petite" Jury list.- *Jury Lists, 1720, Acts #422, [at South Carolina Archives]*, pg. 6.

Holmes, Wm, Male

HOLTON, Thos, - He is on the "Petite" Jury list.- *Jury Lists, 1720, Acts #422, [at South Carolina Archives]*, pg. 8.

Holton, Thos, Male

HOOWARD, Richd, - He is on the Grand Jury list.- *Jury Lists, 1720, Acts #422, [at South Carolina Archives]*, pg. 1.

Hooward, Richd, Male

HORRY, Elias, - He is on the "Petite" Jury list.- *Jury Lists, 1720, Acts #422, [at South Carolina Archives]*, pg. 13.

Horry, Elias, Male
HORRY, Elias, - He is on the Grand Jury list.- *Jury Lists, 1720, Acts #422, [at South Carolina Archives],* pg. 3.
Horry, Elias, Male
HOSER, Henry, - He is on the "Petite" Jury list.- *Jury Lists, 1720, Acts #422, [at South Carolina Archives],* pg. 8.
Hoser, Henry, Male
HOWARD, Thos, - He is on the "Petite" Jury list.- *Jury Lists, 1720, Acts #422, [at South Carolina Archives],* pg. 6.
Howard, Thos, Male
HOWERD, Edwd, - He is on the "Petite" Jury list.- *Jury Lists, 1720, Acts #422, [at South Carolina Archives],* pg. 11.
Howerd, Edwd, Male
HOWES, Robt, - He is on the Grand Jury list.- *Jury Lists, 1720, Acts #422, [at South Carolina Archives],* pg. 3.
Howes, Robt, Male
HOWES, Robt, - He is on the "Petite" Jury list.- *Jury Lists, 1720, Acts #422, [at South Carolina Archives],* pg. 10.
Howes, Robt, Male
HOYDEN, Thos, - He is on the "Petite" Jury list.- *Jury Lists, 1720, Acts #422, [at South Carolina Archives],* pg. 7.
Hoyden, Thos, Male
HUGER, Danle, - He is on the Grand Jury list.- *Jury Lists, 1720, Acts #422, [at South Carolina Archives],* pg. 3.
Huger, Danle, Male
HUGGANS, Jno, - He is on the "Petite" Jury list.- *Jury Lists, 1720, Acts #422, [at South Carolina Archives],* pg. 12.
Huggans, Jno, Male
HUGIER, Danle, - He is on the "Petite" Jury list.- *Jury Lists, 1720, Acts #422, [at South Carolina Archives],* pg. 11.
Hugier, Danle, Male
HYRNE, Edwd, Capt Lieut, - He is on the "Petite" Jury list.- *Jury Lists, 1720, Acts #422, [at South Carolina Archives],* pg. 9.
Hyrne, Edwd, Capt Lieut, Male
HYRNE, Edwd, Capt.Lieut, - He is on the Grand Jury list.- *Jury Lists, 1720, Acts #422, [at South Carolina Archives],* pg. 2.
Hyrne, Edwd, Capt.Lieut, Male

IZARD, Ralph, Esqr, - He is on the Grand Jury list.- *Jury Lists, 1720, Acts #422, [at South Carolina Archives],* pg. 2.
Izard, Ralph, Esqr, Male
IZARD, Ralph, Esqr, - He is on the "Petite" Jury list.- *Jury Lists, 1720, Acts #422, [at South Carolina Archives],* pg. 4.
Izard, Ralph, Esqr, Male
IZARD, Walter, Capt, - He is on the "Petite" Jury list.- *Jury Lists, 1720, Acts #422, [at South Carolina Archives],* pg. 7.
Izard, Walter, Capt, Male
IZARD, Walter, Capt, - He is on the Grand Jury list.- *Jury Lists, 1720, Acts #422, [at South Carolina Archives],* pg. 2.
Izard, Walter, Capt, Male
JACKSON, Henry, - He is on the "Petite" Jury list.- *Jury Lists, 1720, Acts #422, [at South Carolina Archives],* pg. 5.
Jackson, Henry, Male
JACKSON, Jno, - He is on the "Petite" Jury list.- *Jury Lists, 1720, Acts #422, [at South Carolina Archives],* pg. 5.
Jackson, Jno, Male
JACKSON, Jno, - He is on the Grand Jury list.- *Jury Lists, 1720, Acts #422, [at South Carolina Archives],* pg. 1.
Jackson, Jno, Male
JEFFERS, Jno, - He is on the "Petite" Jury list.- *Jury Lists, 1720, Acts #422, [at South Carolina Archives],* pg. 9.
Jeffers, Jno, Male
JENKINS, Jno, - He is on the "Petite" Jury list.- *Jury Lists, 1720, Acts #422, [at South Carolina Archives],* pg. 5.
Jenkins, Jno, Male
JERVIS, Jno, - He is on the "Petite" Jury list.- *Jury Lists, 1720, Acts #422, [at South Carolina Archives],* pg. 4.
Jervis, Jno, Male
JEVEAS?, Jno, Senr, - He is on the "Petite" Jury list.- *Jury Lists, 1720, Acts #422, [at South Carolina Archives],* pg. 13.
Jeveas?, Jno, Senr, Male
JOHNSON, David, - He is on the "Petite" Jury list.- *Jury Lists, 1720, Acts #422, [at South Carolina Archives],* pg. 7.
Johnson, David, Male
JOHNSTON, Petr, Junr, - He is on the "Petite" Jury list.- *Jury Lists, 1720, Acts #422, [at South Carolina Archives],* pg. 12.

Johnston, Petr, Junr, Male
JOHNSTON, Petr, Senr, - He is on the "Petite" Jury list.- *Jury Lists, 1720, Acts #422, [at South Carolina Archives]*, pg. 12.
Johnston, Petr, Senr, Male
JONES, Chas, - He is on the "Petite" Jury list.- *Jury Lists, 1720, Acts #422, [at South Carolina Archives]*, pg. 7.
Jones, Chas, Male
JONES, Jno, - He is on the "Petite" Jury list.- *Jury Lists, 1720, Acts #422, [at South Carolina Archives]*, pg. 10.
Jones, Jno, Male
JONES, Philip, - He is on the "Petite" Jury list.- *Jury Lists, 1720, Acts #422, [at South Carolina Archives]*, pg. 12.
Jones, Philip, Male
JONES, Samle, - He is on the Grand Jury list.- *Jury Lists, 1720, Acts #422, [at South Carolina Archives]*, pg. 1.
Jones, Samle, Male
JONES, Samle, - He is on the "Petite" Jury list.- *Jury Lists, 1720, Acts #422, [at South Carolina Archives]*, pg. 7.
Jones, Samle, Male
JONES, Samle, - He is on the "Petite" Jury list.- *Jury Lists, 1720, Acts #422, [at South Carolina Archives]*, pg. 4.
Jones, Samle, Male
JORDAING, Danle, - He is on the "Petite" Jury list.- *Jury Lists, 1720, Acts #422, [at South Carolina Archives]*, pg. 12.
Jordaing, Danle, Male
KEATON, Edwd, - He is on the "Petite" Jury list.- *Jury Lists, 1720, Acts #422, [at South Carolina Archives]*, pg. 10.
Keaton, Edwd, Male
KELLY, Bryan, - He is on the "Petite" Jury list.- *Jury Lists, 1720, Acts #422, [at South Carolina Archives]*, pg. 5.
Kelly, Bryan, Male
KENLOUGH, Jams, - He is on the "Petite" Jury list.- *Jury Lists, 1720, Acts #422, [at South Carolina Archives]*, pg. 10.
Kenlough, Jams, Male
KING, Edward, - He is on the "Petite" Jury list.- *Jury Lists, 1720, Acts #422, [at South Carolina Archives]*, pg. 6.
King, Edward, Male

KING, Robt, - He is on the Grand Jury list.- *Jury Lists, 1720, Acts #422, [at South Carolina Archives]*, pg. 3.
King, Robt, Male
KING, Robt, - He is on the "Petite" Jury list.- *Jury Lists, 1720, Acts #422, [at South Carolina Archives]*, pg. 12.
King, Robt, Male
KING, Samle, - He is on the "Petite" Jury list.- *Jury Lists, 1720, Acts #422, [at South Carolina Archives]*, pg. 11.
King, Samle, Male
KIRK, Wm, - He is on the "Petite" Jury list.- *Jury Lists, 1720, Acts #422, [at South Carolina Archives]*, pg. 10.
Kirk, Wm, Male
LADSON, Fras, - He is on the "Petite" Jury list.- *Jury Lists, 1720, Acts #422, [at South Carolina Archives]*, pg. 7.
Ladson, Fras, Male
LADSON, Fras, - He is on the Grand Jury list.- *Jury Lists, 1720, Acts #422, [at South Carolina Archives]*, pg. 2.
Ladson, Fras, Male
LADSON, Jacb, - He is on the "Petite" Jury list.- *Jury Lists, 1720, Acts #422, [at South Carolina Archives]*, pg. 7.
Ladson, Jacb, Male
LADSON, Jno, - He is on the "Petite" Jury list.- *Jury Lists, 1720, Acts #422, [at South Carolina Archives]*, pg. 7.
Ladson, Jno, Male
LADSON, Josph, - He is on the "Petite" Jury list.- *Jury Lists, 1720, Acts #422, [at South Carolina Archives]*, pg. 6.
Ladson, Josph, Male
LADSON, Robt, - He is on the "Petite" Jury list.- *Jury Lists, 1720, Acts #422, [at South Carolina Archives]*, pg. 8.
Ladson, Robt, Male
LADSON, Samle, - He is on the "Petite" Jury list.- *Jury Lists, 1720, Acts #422, [at South Carolina Archives]*, pg. 7.
Ladson, Samle, Male
LADSON, Thos, Capt, - He is on the Grand Jury list.- *Jury Lists, 1720, Acts #422, [at South Carolina Archives]*, pg. 1.
Ladson, Thos, Capt, Male
LADSON, Thos, Capt, - He is on the "Petite" Jury list.- *Jury Lists, 1720, Acts #422, [at South Carolina Archives]*, pg. 4.

Ladson, Thos, Capt, Male
LADSON, Wm, - He is on the "Petite" Jury list.- *Jury Lists, 1720, Acts #422, [at South Carolina Archives],* pg. 7.
Ladson, Wm, Male
LAMBOLE, Thos, - He is on the Grand Jury list.- *Jury Lists, 1720, Acts #422, [at South Carolina Archives],* pg. 2.
Lambole, Thos, Male
LAMBOLL, Thos, - He is on the "Petite" Jury list.- *Jury Lists, 1720, Acts #422, [at South Carolina Archives],* pg. 9.
Lamboll, Thos, Male
LANDGRAVE, Thos Smith, - He is on the "Petite" Jury list.- *Jury Lists, 1720, Acts #422, [at South Carolina Archives],* pg. 10.
Landgrave, Thos Smith, Male
LANDGRAVE, Thos Smith, - He is on the Grand Jury list.- *Jury Lists, 1720, Acts #422, [at South Carolina Archives],* pg. 2.
Landgrave, Thos Smith, Male
LANE, Jno, - He is on the "Petite" Jury list.- *Jury Lists, 1720, Acts #422, [at South Carolina Archives],* pg. 13.
Lane, Jno, Male
LARDAN, Jams, - He is on the "Petite" Jury list.- *Jury Lists, 1720, Acts #422, [at South Carolina Archives],* pg. 5.
Lardan, Jams, Male
LAURANCE, Jno, - He is on the "Petite" Jury list.- *Jury Lists, 1720, Acts #422, [at South Carolina Archives],* pg. 9.
Laurance, Jno, Male
LAURANS, - He is on the "Petite" Jury list.- *Jury Lists, 1720, Acts #422, [at South Carolina Archives],* pg. 13.
Laurans, Male
LAW, Josph, - He is on the "Petite" Jury list.- *Jury Lists, 1720, Acts #422, [at South Carolina Archives],* pg. 13.
Law, Josph, Male
LAWSON, Jno, - He is on the "Petite" Jury list.- *Jury Lists, 1720, Acts #422, [at South Carolina Archives],* pg. 11.
Lawson, Jno, Male
LE BRASUER, Fras, - He is on the Grand Jury list.- *Jury Lists, 1720, Acts #422, [at South Carolina Archives],* pg. 2.
Le Brasuer, Fras, Male

LE BRASUER, Fras, - He is on the "Petite" Jury list.- *Jury Lists, 1720, Acts #422, [at South Carolina Archives],* pg. 5.
Le Brasuer, Fras, Male
LE GRAND, Isaac, - He is on the "Petite" Jury list.- *Jury Lists, 1720, Acts #422, [at South Carolina Archives],* pg. 13.
Le Grand, Isaac, Male
LE GRAND, Isaac, - He is on the Grand Jury list.- *Jury Lists, 1720, Acts #422, [at South Carolina Archives],* pg. 3.
Le Grand, Isaac, Male
LE SANE, Isaac, - He is on the "Petite" Jury list.- *Jury Lists, 1720, Acts #422, [at South Carolina Archives],* pg. 12.
Le Sane, Isaac, Male
LEA, Geo, - He is on the "Petite" Jury list.- *Jury Lists, 1720, Acts #422, [at South Carolina Archives],* pg. 9.
Lea, Geo, Male
LEA, Joseph, - He is on the "Petite" Jury list.- *Jury Lists, 1720, Acts #422, [at South Carolina Archives],* pg. 9.
Lea, Joseph, Male
LECOIS, Chas, - He is on the "Petite" Jury list.- *Jury Lists, 1720, Acts #422, [at South Carolina Archives],* pg. 12.
Lecois, Chas, Male
LEGARE, Solon, Senr, - He is on the "Petite" Jury list.- *Jury Lists, 1720, Acts #422, [at South Carolina Archives],* pg. 8.
Legare, Solon, Senr, Male
LEGARE, Solon, Senr, - He is on the Grand Jury list.- *Jury Lists, 1720, Acts #422, [at South Carolina Archives],* pg. 2.
Legare, Solon, Senr, Male
LEGER, Petr, - He is on the "Petite" Jury list.- *Jury Lists, 1720, Acts #422, [at South Carolina Archives],* pg. 13.
Leger, Petr, Male
LEJAU, Fras, Lieut, - He is on the Grand Jury list.- *Jury Lists, 1720, Acts #422, [at South Carolina Archives],* pg. 2.
LeJau, Fras, Lieut, Male
LEJAU, Fras, Lieut, - He is on the "Petite" Jury list.- *Jury Lists, 1720, Acts #422, [at South Carolina Archives],* pg. 9.
LeJau, Fras, Lieut, Male
LEROACH, Jams, - He is on the "Petite" Jury list.- *Jury Lists, 1720, Acts #422, [at South Carolina Archives],* pg. 4.

LeRoach, Jams, Male

LESURR, Josph, - He is on the "Petite" Jury list.- *Jury Lists, 1720, Acts #422, [at South Carolina Archives]*, pg. 6.

Lesurr, Josph, Male

LEVESTON, Geo, - He is on the "Petite" Jury list.- *Jury Lists, 1720, Acts #422, [at South Carolina Archives]*, pg. 11.

Leveston, Geo, Male

LEVESTON, Geo, - He is on the Grand Jury list.- *Jury Lists, 1720, Acts #422, [at South Carolina Archives]*, pg. 3.

Leveston, Geo, Male

LEWIS, Henry, - He is on the "Petite" Jury list.- *Jury Lists, 1720, Acts #422, [at South Carolina Archives]*, pg. 13.

Lewis, Henry, Male

LEWIS, Isaac, Lieut, - He is on the "Petite" Jury list.- *Jury Lists, 1720, Acts #422, [at South Carolina Archives]*, pg. 10.

Lewis, Isaac, Lieut, Male

LISSWARE, Abram, - He is on the "Petite" Jury list.- *Jury Lists, 1720, Acts #422, [at South Carolina Archives]*, pg. 9.

Lissware, Abram, Male

LOGAN, Geo, Colo, - He is on the "Petite" Jury list.- *Jury Lists, 1720, Acts #422, [at South Carolina Archives]*, pg. 12.

Logan, Geo, Colo, Male

LOGAN, Geo, Colo, - He is on the Grand Jury list.- *Jury Lists, 1720, Acts #422, [at South Carolina Archives]*, pg. 3.

Logan, Geo, Colo, Male

LOGAN, Geo, Junr, - He is on the Grand Jury list.- *Jury Lists, 1720, Acts #422, [at South Carolina Archives]*, pg. 3.

Logan, Geo, Junr, Male

LOGAN, Geo, Junr, - He is on the "Petite" Jury list.- *Jury Lists, 1720, Acts #422, [at South Carolina Archives]*, pg. 13.

Logan, Geo, Junr, Male

LOWELL, Samle, - He is on the "Petite" Jury list.- *Jury Lists, 1720, Acts #422, [at South Carolina Archives]*, pg. 4.

Lowell, Samle, Male

LOYD, Thos, - He is on the "Petite" Jury list.- *Jury Lists, 1720, Acts #422, [at South Carolina Archives]*, pg. 8.

Loyd, Thos, Male

LOYD, Thos, - He is on the Grand Jury list.- *Jury Lists, 1720, Acts #422, [at South Carolina Archives]*, pg. 2.

Loyd, Thos, Male

LUCUS, Jams, - He is on the "Petite" Jury list.- *Jury Lists, 1720, Acts #422, [at South Carolina Archives]*, pg. 8.

Lucus, Jams, Male

LYNCH, Thos, Capt, - He is on the "Petite" Jury list.- *Jury Lists, 1720, Acts #422, [at South Carolina Archives]*, pg. 12.

Lynch, Thos, Capt, Male

LYNCH, Thos, Capt, - He is on the Grand Jury list.- *Jury Lists, 1720, Acts #422, [at South Carolina Archives]*, pg. 3.

Lynch, Thos, Capt, Male

MACUNE, Jams, - He is on the "Petite" Jury list.- *Jury Lists, 1720, Acts #422, [at South Carolina Archives]*, pg. 10.

Macune, Jams, Male

MACUNE, Robt, - He is on the "Petite" Jury list.- *Jury Lists, 1720, Acts #422, [at South Carolina Archives]*, pg. 10.

Macune, Robt, Male

MAGGELL, Wm, - He is on the "Petite" Jury list.- *Jury Lists, 1720, Acts #422, [at South Carolina Archives]*, pg. 5.

Maggell, Wm, Male

MAGRIGORY, Danle, - He is on the "Petite" Jury list.- *Jury Lists, 1720, Acts #422, [at South Carolina Archives]*, pg. 13.

Magrigory, Danle, Male

MAIN, Jona, - He is on the "Petite" Jury list.- *Jury Lists, 1720, Acts #422, [at South Carolina Archives]*, pg. 8.

Main, Jona, Male

MAIRJEEK, Isaac, - He is on the Grand Jury list.- *Jury Lists, 1720, Acts #422, [at South Carolina Archives]*, pg. 2.

Mairjeek, Isaac, Male

MAN, Thos, - He is on the "Petite" Jury list.- *Jury Lists, 1720, Acts #422, [at South Carolina Archives]*, pg. 7.

Man, Thos, Male

MANIGAULT, Peter, - He is on the "Petite" Jury list.- *Jury Lists, 1720, Acts #422, [at South Carolina Archives]*, pg. 9.

Manigault, Peter, Male

MANIGAULT, Peter, - He is on the Grand Jury list.- *Jury Lists, 1720, Acts #422, [at South Carolina Archives]*, pg. 2.

Manigault, Peter, Male
MARBUFF, Josph, - He is on the "Petite" Jury list.- *Jury Lists, 1720, Acts #422, [at South Carolina Archives],* pg. 12.
   Marbuff, Josph, Male
MARCHANT, Rene, - He is on the "Petite" Jury list.- *Jury Lists, 1720, Acts #422, [at South Carolina Archives],* pg. 10.
   Marchant, Rene, Male
MARINER, Joshua, - He is on the "Petite" Jury list.- *Jury Lists, 1720, Acts #422, [at South Carolina Archives],* pg. 9.
   Mariner, Joshua, Male
MARION, Gabriel, - He is on the Grand Jury list.- *Jury Lists, 1720, Acts #422, [at South Carolina Archives],* pg. 3.
   Marion, Gabriel, Male
MARION, Gabriel, - He is on the "Petite" Jury list.- *Jury Lists, 1720, Acts #422, [at South Carolina Archives],* pg. 14.
   Marion, Gabriel, Male
MARQUESS, Emanuel, - He is on the "Petite" Jury list.- *Jury Lists, 1720, Acts #422, [at South Carolina Archives],* pg. 4.
   Marquess, Emanuel, Male
MARRION, Benja, - He is on the Grand Jury list.- *Jury Lists, 1720, Acts #422, [at South Carolina Archives],* pg. 2.
   Marrion, Benja, Male
MARRION, Benja, - He is on the "Petite" Jury list.- *Jury Lists, 1720, Acts #422, [at South Carolina Archives],* pg. 10.
   Marrion, Benja, Male
MARTIAL, Jno, - He is on the "Petite" Jury list.- *Jury Lists, 1720, Acts #422, [at South Carolina Archives],* pg. 4.
   Martial, Jno, Male
MARTIN, Moses, - He is on the "Petite" Jury list.- *Jury Lists, 1720, Acts #422, [at South Carolina Archives],* pg. 5.
   Martin, Moses, Male
MASHEW, Henry, - He is on the "Petite" Jury list.- *Jury Lists, 1720, Acts #422, [at South Carolina Archives],* pg. 5.
   Mashew, Henry, Male
MASON, Richd, - He is on the "Petite" Jury list.- *Jury Lists, 1720, Acts #422, [at South Carolina Archives],* pg. 14.
   Mason, Richd, Male

MASSEY, Josph, - He is on the "Petite" Jury list.- *Jury Lists, 1720, Acts #422, [at South Carolina Archives],* pg. 8.
   Massey, Josph, Male
MASTERS, Samle, - He is on the "Petite" Jury list.- *Jury Lists, 1720, Acts #422, [at South Carolina Archives],* pg. 13.
   Masters, Samle, Male
MATHEWS, Antho, - He is on the Grand Jury list.- *Jury Lists, 1720, Acts #422, [at South Carolina Archives],* pg. 2.
   Mathews, Antho, Male
MATHEWS, Antho, - He is on the "Petite" Jury list.- *Jury Lists, 1720, Acts #422, [at South Carolina Archives],* pg. 9.
   Mathews, Antho, Male
MAYRANT, Jams Nichs, - He is on the "Petite" Jury list.- *Jury Lists, 1720, Acts #422, [at South Carolina Archives],* pg. 13.
   Mayrant, Jams Nichs, Male
MCCLENAN, - He is on the "Petite" Jury list.- *Jury Lists, 1720, Acts #422, [at South Carolina Archives],* pg. 11.
   McClenan, Male
MCCLOCKLIN, Jams, - He is on the "Petite" Jury list.- *Jury Lists, 1720, Acts #422, [at South Carolina Archives],* pg. 7.
   McClocklin, Jams, Male
MCLES, Jno, Ensigne, - He is on the "Petite" Jury list.- *Jury Lists, 1720, Acts #422, [at South Carolina Archives],* pg. 6.
   Mcles, Jno, Ensigne, Male
MEADS, Wm, - He is on the "Petite" Jury list.- *Jury Lists, 1720, Acts #422, [at South Carolina Archives],* pg. 8.
   Meads, Wm, Male
MELVIN, Jno, - He is on the "Petite" Jury list.- *Jury Lists, 1720, Acts #422, [at South Carolina Archives],* pg. 5.
   Melvin, Jno, Male
MEREDAY, Josph, - He is on the "Petite" Jury list.- *Jury Lists, 1720, Acts #422, [at South Carolina Archives],* pg. 4.
   Mereday, Josph, Male
MICHALL, Ephraim, - He is on the "Petite" Jury list.- *Jury Lists, 1720, Acts #422, [at South Carolina Archives],* pg. 5.
   Michall, Ephraim, Male
MIDDLETON, Arthr, - He is on the Grand Jury list.- *Jury Lists, 1720, Acts #422, [at South Carolina Archives],* pg. 3.

Middleton, Arthr, Male

MIDDLETON, Arthur, Esqr, - He is on the "Petite" Jury list.- *Jury Lists, 1720, Acts #422, [at South Carolina Archives]*, pg. 10.

Middleton, Arthur, Esqr, Male

MILES, Jeremiah, - He is on the "Petite" Jury list.- *Jury Lists, 1720, Acts #422, [at South Carolina Archives]*, pg. 4.

Miles, Jeremiah, Male

MILES, Thos, - He is on the "Petite" Jury list.- *Jury Lists, 1720, Acts #422, [at South Carolina Archives]*, pg. 4.

Miles, Thos, Male

MILES, Wm, - He is on the "Petite" Jury list.- *Jury Lists, 1720, Acts #422, [at South Carolina Archives]*, pg. 7.

Miles, Wm, Male

MILLER, Robt, Senr, - He is on the "Petite" Jury list.- *Jury Lists, 1720, Acts #422, [at South Carolina Archives]*, pg. 8.

Miller, Robt, Senr, Male

MILLER, Samle, - He is on the "Petite" Jury list.- *Jury Lists, 1720, Acts #422, [at South Carolina Archives]*, pg. 13.

Miller, Samle, Male

MILLS, Thos, - He is on the "Petite" Jury list.- *Jury Lists, 1720, Acts #422, [at South Carolina Archives]*, pg. 10.

Mills, Thos, Male

MILNER, Jno, - He is on the "Petite" Jury list.- *Jury Lists, 1720, Acts #422, [at South Carolina Archives]*, pg. 8.

Milner, Jno, Male

MILNER, Jona, - He is on the "Petite" Jury list.- *Jury Lists, 1720, Acts #422, [at South Carolina Archives]*, pg. 13.

Milner, Jona, Male

MITCHELL, Geo, - He is on the "Petite" Jury list.- *Jury Lists, 1720, Acts #422, [at South Carolina Archives]*, pg. 5.

Mitchell, Geo, Male

MONGER, Garrard, - He is on the "Petite" Jury list.- *Jury Lists, 1720, Acts #422, [at South Carolina Archives]*, pg. 7.

Monger, Garrard, Male

MONGER, Garrard, - He is on the Grand Jury list.- *Jury Lists, 1720, Acts #422, [at South Carolina Archives]*, pg. 2.

Monger, Garrard, Male

MOORE, Roger, - He is on the Grand Jury list.- *Jury Lists, 1720, Acts #422, [at South Carolina Archives]*, pg. 3.

Moore, Roger, Male

MOORE, Roger, - He is on the "Petite" Jury list.- *Jury Lists, 1720, Acts #422, [at South Carolina Archives]*, pg. 10.

Moore, Roger, Male

MOORE ALIAS GOFEL, Jno, - He is on the Grand Jury list.- *Jury Lists, 1720, Acts #422, [at South Carolina Archives]*, pg. 3.

Moore alias Gofel, Jno, Male

MOORE ALIAS GUPHEL, Jno, - He is on the "Petite" Jury list.- *Jury Lists, 1720, Acts #422, [at South Carolina Archives]*, pg. 11.

Moore Alias Guphel, Jno, Male

MORRIS, Thos, - He is on the "Petite" Jury list.- *Jury Lists, 1720, Acts #422, [at South Carolina Archives]*, pg. 7.

Morris, Thos, Male

MORTON, Landgrave, - He is on the "Petite" Jury list.- *Jury Lists, 1720, Acts #422, [at South Carolina Archives]*, pg. 4.

Morton, Landgrave, Male

MORTON, Landgrave, - He is on the Grand Jury list.- *Jury Lists, 1720, Acts #422, [at South Carolina Archives]*, pg. 1.

Morton, Landgrave, Male

MOUZON, Lewis, - He is on the "Petite" Jury list.- *Jury Lists, 1720, Acts #422, [at South Carolina Archives]*, pg. 11.

Mouzon, Lewis, Male

MURPHY, Mauries, - He is on the "Petite" Jury list.- *Jury Lists, 1720, Acts #422, [at South Carolina Archives]*, pg. 13.

Murphy, Mauries, Male

MURRIL, Jno, - He is on the "Petite" Jury list.- *Jury Lists, 1720, Acts #422, [at South Carolina Archives]*, pg. 13.

Murril, Jno, Male

MURRIL, Jno, - He is on the "Petite" Jury list.- *Jury Lists, 1720, Acts #422, [at South Carolina Archives]*, pg. 13.

Murril, Jno, Male, Cooper

MURRIL, Jona, - He is on the "Petite" Jury list.- *Jury Lists, 1720, Acts #422, [at South Carolina Archives]*, pg. 13.

Murril, Jona, Male

MURRIL, Wm, - He is on the "Petite" Jury list.- *Jury Lists, 1720, Acts #422, [at South Carolina Archives]*, pg. 13.

Murril, Wm, Male
NASH, Thos, - He is on the "Petite" Jury list.- *Jury Lists, 1720, Acts #422, [at South Carolina Archives]*, pg. 4.
Nash, Thos, Male
NICHOLS, Henry, - He is on the "Petite" Jury list.- *Jury Lists, 1720, Acts #422, [at South Carolina Archives]*, pg. 4.
Nichols, Henry, Male
NICHOLS, Nathle, - He is on the "Petite" Jury list.- *Jury Lists, 1720, Acts #422, [at South Carolina Archives]*, pg. 4.
Nichols, Nathle, Male
NORMAN, Moses, - He is on the "Petite" Jury list.- *Jury Lists, 1720, Acts #422, [at South Carolina Archives]*, pg. 8.
Norman, Moses, Male
NORMAN, Wm, - He is on the "Petite" Jury list.- *Jury Lists, 1720, Acts #422, [at South Carolina Archives]*, pg. 10.
Norman, Wm, Male
NORMAND, Petr, - He is on the "Petite" Jury list.- *Jury Lists, 1720, Acts #422, [at South Carolina Archives]*, pg. 12.
Normand, Petr, Male
NORTH, Edwd, - He is on the "Petite" Jury list.- *Jury Lists, 1720, Acts #422, [at South Carolina Archives]*, pg. 5.
North, Edwd, Male
OLDFIELD, Jno, - He is on the "Petite" Jury list.- *Jury Lists, 1720, Acts #422, [at South Carolina Archives]*, pg. 9.
Oldfield, Jno, Male
OLDFIELD, John, - He is on the Grand Jury list.- *Jury Lists, 1720, Acts #422, [at South Carolina Archives]*, pg. 2.
Oldfield, John, Male
OLDRIGE, Josph, - He is on the "Petite" Jury list.- *Jury Lists, 1720, Acts #422, [at South Carolina Archives]*, pg. 5.
Oldrige, Josph, Male
OLIVER, Bartho, - He is on the "Petite" Jury list.- *Jury Lists, 1720, Acts #422, [at South Carolina Archives]*, pg. 9.
Oliver, Bartho, Male
OSGOOD, Josia, - He is on the "Petite" Jury list.- *Jury Lists, 1720, Acts #422, [at South Carolina Archives]*, pg. 8.
Osgood, Josia, Male

OSGOOD, Thos, Junr, - He is on the "Petite" Jury list.- *Jury Lists, 1720, Acts #422, [at South Carolina Archives]*, pg. 8.
Osgood, Thos, Junr, Male
OSWELL, Wm, - He is on the "Petite" Jury list.- *Jury Lists, 1720, Acts #422, [at South Carolina Archives]*, pg. 5.
Oswell, Wm, Male
OWEN, Philip, - He is on the "Petite" Jury list.- *Jury Lists, 1720, Acts #422, [at South Carolina Archives]*, pg. 4.
Owen, Philip, Male
PAGITT, Fras, Senr, - He is on the "Petite" Jury list.- *Jury Lists, 1720, Acts #422, [at South Carolina Archives]*, pg. 12.
Pagitt, Fras, Senr, Male
PAIR, David, - He is on the "Petite" Jury list.- *Jury Lists, 1720, Acts #422, [at South Carolina Archives]*, pg. 11.
Pair, David, Male
PALLY, Geo, - He is on the "Petite" Jury list.- *Jury Lists, 1720, Acts #422, [at South Carolina Archives]*, pg. 10.
Pally, Geo, Male
PALMER, Jno, - He is on the "Petite" Jury list.- *Jury Lists, 1720, Acts #422, [at South Carolina Archives]*, pg. 4.
Palmer, Jno, Male
PALMER, Jno, - He is on the Grand Jury list.- *Jury Lists, 1720, Acts #422, [at South Carolina Archives]*, pg. 1.
Palmer, Jno, Male
PALMER, Jona, - He is on the "Petite" Jury list.- *Jury Lists, 1720, Acts #422, [at South Carolina Archives]*, pg. 11.
Palmer, Jona, Male
PALMER, Thos, - He is on the "Petite" Jury list.- *Jury Lists, 1720, Acts #422, [at South Carolina Archives]*, pg. 10.
Palmer, Thos, Male
PALMERTER, Josph, - He is on the "Petite" Jury list.- *Jury Lists, 1720, Acts #422, [at South Carolina Archives]*, pg. 5.
Palmerter, Josph, Male
PALMETER, Peter, - He is on the "Petite" Jury list.- *Jury Lists, 1720, Acts #422, [at South Carolina Archives]*, pg. 5.
Palmeter, Peter, Male
PARKER, Jno, - He is on the "Petite" Jury list.- *Jury Lists, 1720, Acts #422, [at South Carolina Archives]*, pg. 9.

Parker, Jno, Male

PARKER, Jno, - He is on the Grand Jury list.- *Jury Lists, 1720, Acts #422, [at South Carolina Archives]*, pg. 2.

Parker, Jno, Male

PARRIS, Alexr, Colo, - He is on the "Petite" Jury list.- *Jury Lists, 1720, Acts #422, [at South Carolina Archives]*, pg. 9.

Parris, Alexr, Colo, Male

PARRIS, Allexr, Junr, - He is on the "Petite" Jury list.- *Jury Lists, 1720, Acts #422, [at South Carolina Archives]*, pg. 3.

Parris, Allexr, Junr, Male

PARRIS, Colo, - He is on the Grand Jury list.- *Jury Lists, 1720, Acts #422, [at South Carolina Archives]*, pg. 2.

Parris, Colo, Male

PARRIS, Peter, - He is on the "Petite" Jury list.- *Jury Lists, 1720, Acts #422, [at South Carolina Archives]*, pg. 9.

Parris, Peter, Male

PEACOCK, Thos, - He is on the "Petite" Jury list.- *Jury Lists, 1720, Acts #422, [at South Carolina Archives]*, pg. 11.

Peacock, Thos, Male

PECKHAM, Jos, - He is on the "Petite" Jury list.- *Jury Lists, 1720, Acts #422, [at South Carolina Archives]*, pg. 5.

Peckham, Jos, Male

PENDARVIS, Jno, - He is on the "Petite" Jury list.- *Jury Lists, 1720, Acts #422, [at South Carolina Archives]*, pg. 7.

Pendarvis, Jno, Male

PENDARVIS, Jno, - He is on the Grand Jury list.- *Jury Lists, 1720, Acts #422, [at South Carolina Archives]*, pg. 2.

Pendarvis, Jno, Male

PENDARVIS, Josph, - He is on the "Petite" Jury list.- *Jury Lists, 1720, Acts #422, [at South Carolina Archives]*, pg. 7.

Pendarvis, Josph, Male

PERDRIAU, Petr, - He is on the "Petite" Jury list.- *Jury Lists, 1720, Acts #422, [at South Carolina Archives]*, pg. 13.

Perdriau, Petr, Male

PERREY, Benja, - He is on the "Petite" Jury list.- *Jury Lists, 1720, Acts #422, [at South Carolina Archives]*, pg. 7.

Perrey, Benja, Male

PERRINEAU, Henry, - He is on the "Petite" Jury list.- *Jury Lists, 1720, Acts #422, [at South Carolina Archives]*, pg. 9.

Perrineau, Henry, Male

PETERS, Jno, - He is on the "Petite" Jury list.- *Jury Lists, 1720, Acts #422, [at South Carolina Archives]*, pg. 5.

Peters, Jno, Male

PETERSON, Geo, - He is on the "Petite" Jury list.- *Jury Lists, 1720, Acts #422, [at South Carolina Archives]*, pg. 14.

Peterson, Geo, Male

PHRIP, Jno, - He is on the "Petite" Jury list.- *Jury Lists, 1720, Acts #422, [at South Carolina Archives]*, pg. 5.

Phrip, Jno, Male

PICKERING, Samle, - He is on the Grand Jury list.- *Jury Lists, 1720, Acts #422, [at South Carolina Archives]*, pg. 3.

Pickering, Samle, Male

PICKERING, Samle, - He is on the "Petite" Jury list.- *Jury Lists, 1720, Acts #422, [at South Carolina Archives]*, pg. 10.

Pickering, Samle, Male

PLAYER, Rogr, - He is on the "Petite" Jury list.- *Jury Lists, 1720, Acts #422, [at South Carolina Archives]*, pg. 13.

Player, Rogr, Male

PLOMAN, Mark, - He is on the "Petite" Jury list.- *Jury Lists, 1720, Acts #422, [at South Carolina Archives]*, pg. 13.

Ploman, Mark, Male

PLUMMER, Moses, - He is on the "Petite" Jury list.- *Jury Lists, 1720, Acts #422, [at South Carolina Archives]*, pg. 12.

Plummer, Moses, Male

POITEVAIN, Antho, - He is on the "Petite" Jury list.- *Jury Lists, 1720, Acts #422, [at South Carolina Archives]*, pg. 11.

Poitevain, Antho, Male

PONTOIX, Zach, - He is on the "Petite" Jury list.- *Jury Lists, 1720, Acts #422, [at South Carolina Archives]*, pg. 10.

Pontoix, Zach, Male

PORCHER, Peter, - He is on the "Petite" Jury list.- *Jury Lists, 1720, Acts #422, [at South Carolina Archives]*, pg. 10.

Porcher, Peter, Male

PORTER, Edmund, - He is on the "Petite" Jury list.- *Jury Lists, 1720, Acts #422, [at South Carolina Archives]*, pg. 9.

Porter, Edmund, Male

PORTEVINE, Petr, - He is on the "Petite" Jury list.- *Jury Lists, 1720, Acts #422, [at South Carolina Archives],* pg. 11.

Portevine, Petr, Male

PRIELEAU, Elisha, - He is on the "Petite" Jury list.- *Jury Lists, 1720, Acts #422, [at South Carolina Archives],* pg. 9.

Prieleau, Elisha, Male

PRIELEAU, Elisha, - He is on the Grand Jury list.- *Jury Lists, 1720, Acts #422, [at South Carolina Archives],* pg. 2.

Prieleau, Elisha, Male

PRIMBOLL, Thoms, - He is on the Grand Jury list.- *Jury Lists, 1720, Acts #422, [at South Carolina Archives],* pg. 1.

Primboll, Thoms, Male

PYNEY, Jno, - He is on the "Petite" Jury list.- *Jury Lists, 1720, Acts #422, [at South Carolina Archives],* pg. 4.

Pyney, Jno, Male

QUELCH, Benja, - He is on the "Petite" Jury list.- *Jury Lists, 1720, Acts #422, [at South Carolina Archives],* pg. 13.

Quelch, Benja, Male

RAMACK, Isaac, - He is on the "Petite" Jury list.- *Jury Lists, 1720, Acts #422, [at South Carolina Archives],* pg. 3.

Ramack, Isaac, Male

RAMSEY, Jno, - He is on the "Petite" Jury list.- *Jury Lists, 1720, Acts #422, [at South Carolina Archives],* pg. 8.

Ramsey, Jno, Male

RAUGHMALLER, Job, - He is on the "Petite" Jury list.- *Jury Lists, 1720, Acts #422, [at South Carolina Archives],* pg. 9.

Raughmaller, Job, Male

RAVEN, Jno, - He is on the "Petite" Jury list.- *Jury Lists, 1720, Acts #422, [at South Carolina Archives],* pg. 3.

Raven, Jno, Male

RAVEN, Jno, - He is on the Grand Jury list.- *Jury Lists, 1720, Acts #422, [at South Carolina Archives],* pg. 1.

Raven, Jno, Male

RAVENEL, Danle, - He is on the "Petite" Jury list.- *Jury Lists, 1720, Acts #422, [at South Carolina Archives],* pg. 10.

Ravenel, Danle, Male

RAVENEL, Paul, - He is on the "Petite" Jury list.- *Jury Lists, 1720, Acts #422, [at South Carolina Archives],* pg. 10.

Ravenel, Paul, Male

RAVENEL, Rene, - He is on the "Petite" Jury list.- *Jury Lists, 1720, Acts #422, [at South Carolina Archives],* pg. 10.

Ravenel, Rene, Male

RAVENELL, Danle, - He is on the Grand Jury list.- *Jury Lists, 1720, Acts #422, [at South Carolina Archives],* pg. 3.

Ravenell, Danle, Male

RAVENELL, Rene, - He is on the Grand Jury list.- *Jury Lists, 1720, Acts #422, [at South Carolina Archives],* pg. 3.

Ravenell, Rene, Male

RAWLINGS, Jams, - He is on the "Petite" Jury list.- *Jury Lists, 1720, Acts #422, [at South Carolina Archives],* pg. 7.

Rawlings, Jams, Male

REALY, Barnaby, - He is on the "Petite" Jury list.- *Jury Lists, 1720, Acts #422, [at South Carolina Archives],* pg. 10.

Realy, Barnaby, Male

RENOLDS, Richd, - He is on the "Petite" Jury list.- *Jury Lists, 1720, Acts #422, [at South Carolina Archives],* pg. 5.

Renolds, Richd, Male

RENOLS, Michael, - He is on the "Petite" Jury list.- *Jury Lists, 1720, Acts #422, [at South Carolina Archives],* pg. 4.

Renols, Michael, Male

RHETT, Wm, Colo, - He is on the "Petite" Jury list.- *Jury Lists, 1720, Acts #422, [at South Carolina Archives],* pg. 4.

Rhett, Wm, Colo, Male

RHETT, Wm, Colo, - He is on the Grand Jury list.- *Jury Lists, 1720, Acts #422, [at South Carolina Archives],* pg. 1.

Rhett, Wm, Colo, Male

RIBBES, Jno, - He is on the "Petite" Jury list.- *Jury Lists, 1720, Acts #422, [at South Carolina Archives],* pg. 9.

Ribbes, Jno, Male

RIEN, Miles, - He is on the "Petite" Jury list.- *Jury Lists, 1720, Acts #422, [at South Carolina Archives],* pg. 4.

Rien, Miles, Male

RIGGS, Wm, - He is on the "Petite" Jury list.- *Jury Lists, 1720, Acts #422, [at South Carolina Archives],* pg. 10.

Riggs, Wm, Male

RIVERS, Geo, - He is on the "Petite" Jury list.- *Jury Lists, 1720, Acts #422, [at South Carolina Archives]*, pg. 6.

Rivers, Geo, Male

RIVERS, Geo, - He is on the Grand Jury list.- *Jury Lists, 1720, Acts #422, [at South Carolina Archives]*, pg. 1.

Rivers, Geo, Male

RIVERS, Jeremiah, - He is on the "Petite" Jury list.- *Jury Lists, 1720, Acts #422, [at South Carolina Archives]*, pg. 6.

Rivers, Jeremiah, Male

RIVERS, Josph, - He is on the "Petite" Jury list.- *Jury Lists, 1720, Acts #422, [at South Carolina Archives]*, pg. 6.

Rivers, Josph, Male

RIVERS, Miles, - He is on the "Petite" Jury list.- *Jury Lists, 1720, Acts #422, [at South Carolina Archives]*, pg. 7.

Rivers, Miles, Male

RIVERS, Richd, - He is on the "Petite" Jury list.- *Jury Lists, 1720, Acts #422, [at South Carolina Archives]*, pg. 6.

Rivers, Richd, Male

ROBERT, Petr, - He is on the Grand Jury list.- *Jury Lists, 1720, Acts #422, [at South Carolina Archives]*, pg. 3.

Robert, Petr, Male

ROBERTS, Jno, - He is on the "Petite" Jury list.- *Jury Lists, 1720, Acts #422, [at South Carolina Archives]*, pg. 4.

Roberts, Jno, Male

ROBERTS, Petr, - He is on the "Petite" Jury list.- *Jury Lists, 1720, Acts #422, [at South Carolina Archives]*, pg. 13.

Roberts, Petr, Male

ROBINSON, Jams, - He is on the "Petite" Jury list.- *Jury Lists, 1720, Acts #422, [at South Carolina Archives]*, pg. 11.

Robinson, Jams, Male

ROPER, Jeremiah, - He is on the "Petite" Jury list.- *Jury Lists, 1720, Acts #422, [at South Carolina Archives]*, pg. 12.

Roper, Jeremiah, Male

ROPER, Josph, - He is on the "Petite" Jury list.- *Jury Lists, 1720, Acts #422, [at South Carolina Archives]*, pg. 12.

Roper, Josph, Male

ROSE, Thos, - He is on the "Petite" Jury list.- *Jury Lists, 1720, Acts #422, [at South Carolina Archives]*, pg. 6.

Rose, Thos, Male

ROW, Richd, - He is on the "Petite" Jury list.- *Jury Lists, 1720, Acts #422, [at South Carolina Archives]*, pg. 11.

Row, Richd, Male

ROWLAND, Josph, - He is on the "Petite" Jury list.- *Jury Lists, 1720, Acts #422, [at South Carolina Archives]*, pg. 10.

Rowland, Josph, Male

ROWSER, Richd, - He is on the "Petite" Jury list.- *Jury Lists, 1720, Acts #422, [at South Carolina Archives]*, pg. 12.

Rowser, Richd, Male

RUSKO, Samle, - He is on the "Petite" Jury list.- *Jury Lists, 1720, Acts #422, [at South Carolina Archives]*, pg. 14.

Rusko, Samle, Male

RUSS, Jona, Senr, - He is on the "Petite" Jury list.- *Jury Lists, 1720, Acts #422, [at South Carolina Archives]*, pg. 12.

Russ, Jona, Senr, Male

RUSSELL, Josph, - He is on the "Petite" Jury list.- *Jury Lists, 1720, Acts #422, [at South Carolina Archives]*, pg. 5.

Russell, Josph, Male

RUSSELL, Stephen, - He is on the "Petite" Jury list.- *Jury Lists, 1720, Acts #422, [at South Carolina Archives]*, pg. 6.

Russell, Stephen, Male

SAELLENS, Petr, - He is on the "Petite" Jury list.- *Jury Lists, 1720, Acts #422, [at South Carolina Archives]*, pg. 11.

Saellens, Petr, Male

SAMS, Jno, - He is on the "Petite" Jury list.- *Jury Lists, 1720, Acts #422, [at South Carolina Archives]*, pg. 5.

Sams, Jno, Male

SANDERS, Jno, - He is on the "Petite" Jury list.- *Jury Lists, 1720, Acts #422, [at South Carolina Archives]*, pg. 9.

Sanders, Jno, Male

SANDERS, Jno, - He is on the Grand Jury list.- *Jury Lists, 1720, Acts #422, [at South Carolina Archives]*, pg. 2.

Sanders, Jno, Male

SANDERS, Joshua, - He is on the "Petite" Jury list.- *Jury Lists, 1720, Acts #422, [at South Carolina Archives]*, pg. 10.

Sanders, Joshua, Male

SANDERS, Petr, - He is on the "Petite" Jury list.- *Jury Lists, 1720, Acts #422, [at South Carolina Archives],* pg. 13.

Sanders, Petr, Male

SANDERS, Samle, - He is on the "Petite" Jury list.- *Jury Lists, 1720, Acts #422, [at South Carolina Archives],* pg. 14.

Sanders, Samle, Male

SANDERS, Wilson, - He is on the "Petite" Jury list.- *Jury Lists, 1720, Acts #422, [at South Carolina Archives],* pg. 10.

Sanders, Wilson, Male

SANDIFORD, Jno, - He is on the "Petite" Jury list.- *Jury Lists, 1720, Acts #422, [at South Carolina Archives],* pg. 6.

Sandiford, Jno, Male

SANSEAU, Jno, - He is on the "Petite" Jury list.- *Jury Lists, 1720, Acts #422, [at South Carolina Archives],* pg. 12.

Sanseau, Jno, Male

SATUR, Thos, - He is on the "Petite" Jury list.- *Jury Lists, 1720, Acts #422, [at South Carolina Archives],* pg. 7.

Satur, Thos, Male

SATUR?, Thos, - He is on the Grand Jury list.- *Jury Lists, 1720, Acts #422, [at South Carolina Archives],* pg. 2.

Satur?, Thos, Male

SAUNDERS, Jno, - He is on the "Petite" Jury list.- *Jury Lists, 1720, Acts #422, [at South Carolina Archives],* pg. 12.

Saunders, Jno, Male

SAUNDERS, Roger, - He is on the "Petite" Jury list.- *Jury Lists, 1720, Acts #422, [at South Carolina Archives],* pg. 10.

Saunders, Roger, Male

SAUNDERS, Rogr, - He is on the Grand Jury list.- *Jury Lists, 1720, Acts #422, [at South Carolina Archives],* pg. 3.

Saunders, Rogr, Male

SAUNDERS, Wm, - He is on the "Petite" Jury list.- *Jury Lists, 1720, Acts #422, [at South Carolina Archives],* pg. 7.

Saunders, Wm, Male

SAUNDERS, Wm, - He is on the Grand Jury list.- *Jury Lists, 1720, Acts #422, [at South Carolina Archives],* pg. 2.

Saunders, Wm, Male

SAVINEAU, Jams, - He is on the "Petite" Jury list.- *Jury Lists, 1720, Acts #422, [at South Carolina Archives],* pg. 11.

Savineau, Jams, Male

SAXBY, Antho, - He is on the "Petite" Jury list.- *Jury Lists, 1720, Acts #422, [at South Carolina Archives],* pg. 5.

Saxby, Antho, Male

SCHENCKINGLE?, Benja, - He is on the Grand Jury list.- *Jury Lists, 1720, Acts #422, [at South Carolina Archives],* pg. 2.

Schenckingle?, Benja, Male

SCHENEKINGH, Benja, - He is on the "Petite" Jury list.- *Jury Lists, 1720, Acts #422, [at South Carolina Archives],* pg. 10.

Schenekingh, Benja, Male

SCOTT, Jams, - He is on the "Petite" Jury list.- *Jury Lists, 1720, Acts #422, [at South Carolina Archives],* pg. 5.

Scott, Jams, Male

SCOTT, Josph, - He is on the "Petite" Jury list.- *Jury Lists, 1720, Acts #422, [at South Carolina Archives],* pg. 5.

Scott, Josph, Male

SCOTT, Wm, Capt, - He is on the "Petite" Jury list.- *Jury Lists, 1720, Acts #422, [at South Carolina Archives],* pg. 4.

Scott, Wm, Capt, Male

SCOTT, Wm, Capt, - He is on the Grand Jury list.- *Jury Lists, 1720, Acts #422, [at South Carolina Archives],* pg. 1.

Scott, Wm, Capt, Male

SEABROOK, Jos, - He is on the "Petite" Jury list.- *Jury Lists, 1720, Acts #422, [at South Carolina Archives],* pg. 5.

Seabrook, Jos, Male

SEABROOK, Robt, - He is on the "Petite" Jury list.- *Jury Lists, 1720, Acts #422, [at South Carolina Archives],* pg. 4.

Seabrook, Robt, Male

SEALY, Jos, - He is on the "Petite" Jury list.- *Jury Lists, 1720, Acts #422, [at South Carolina Archives],* pg. 5.

Sealy, Jos, Male

SERIVEN, Elisha, - He is on the "Petite" Jury list.- *Jury Lists, 1720, Acts #422, [at South Carolina Archives],* pg. 13.

Seriven, Elisha, Male

SERMAN, Josph, - He is on the "Petite" Jury list.- *Jury Lists, 1720, Acts #422, [at South Carolina Archives],* pg. 6.

Serman, Josph, Male

SERMAN, Samle, - He is on the "Petite" Jury list.- *Jury Lists, 1720, Acts #422, [at South Carolina Archives],* pg. 6.

Serman, Samle, Male

SERMAN, Samle, - He is on the Grand Jury list.- *Jury Lists, 1720, Acts #422, [at South Carolina Archives],* pg. 1.

Serman, Samle, Male

SERRY, Noah, - He is on the Grand Jury list.- *Jury Lists, 1720, Acts #422, [at South Carolina Archives],* pg. 3.

Serry, Noah, Male

SERY, Noah, - He is on the "Petite" Jury list.- *Jury Lists, 1720, Acts #422, [at South Carolina Archives],* pg. 13.

Sery, Noah, Male

SEVERENSE, Jno, - He is on the "Petite" Jury list.- *Jury Lists, 1720, Acts #422, [at South Carolina Archives],* pg. 13.

Severense, Jno, Male

SHAW, Jno, - He is on the "Petite" Jury list.- *Jury Lists, 1720, Acts #422, [at South Carolina Archives],* pg. 13.

Shaw, Jno, Male

SHEENE, Alexr, Esqr, - He is on the Grand Jury list.- *Jury Lists, 1720, Acts #422, [at South Carolina Archives],* pg. 2.

Sheene, Alexr, Esqr, Male

SHEPHERD, Jno, - He is on the "Petite" Jury list.- *Jury Lists, 1720, Acts #422, [at South Carolina Archives],* pg. 8.

Shepherd, Jno, Male

SHERIFF, Henry, - He is on the "Petite" Jury list.- *Jury Lists, 1720, Acts #422, [at South Carolina Archives],* pg. 4.

Sheriff, Henry, Male

SHINGLETON, Richd, - He is on the "Petite" Jury list.- *Jury Lists, 1720, Acts #422, [at South Carolina Archives],* pg. 10.

Shingleton, Richd, Male

SHINGLETON, Wm, - He is on the "Petite" Jury list.- *Jury Lists, 1720, Acts #422, [at South Carolina Archives],* pg. 5.

Shingleton, Wm, Male

SHIPPER, Wm, - He is on the "Petite" Jury list.- *Jury Lists, 1720, Acts #422, [at South Carolina Archives],* pg. 6.

Shipper, Wm, Male

SIBBLEY, Wm, - He is on the "Petite" Jury list.- *Jury Lists, 1720, Acts #422, [at South Carolina Archives],* pg. 13.

Sibbley, Wm, Male

SIMMONS, Fras, - He is on the "Petite" Jury list.- *Jury Lists, 1720, Acts #422, [at South Carolina Archives],* pg. 11.

Simmons, Fras, Male

SIMMONS, Henry, - He is on the "Petite" Jury list.- *Jury Lists, 1720, Acts #422, [at South Carolina Archives],* pg. 14.

Simmons, Henry, Male

SIMMONS, Henry, - He is on the "Petite" Jury list.- *Jury Lists, 1720, Acts #422, [at South Carolina Archives],* pg. 10.

Simmons, Henry, Male

SIMMONS, Jno, - He is on the "Petite" Jury list.- *Jury Lists, 1720, Acts #422, [at South Carolina Archives],* pg. 8.

Simmons, Jno, Male

SIMMONS, Peter, - He is on the "Petite" Jury list.- *Jury Lists, 1720, Acts #422, [at South Carolina Archives],* pg. 14.

Simmons, Peter, Male

SIMMONS, Samle, - He is on the "Petite" Jury list.- *Jury Lists, 1720, Acts #422, [at South Carolina Archives],* pg. 14.

Simmons, Samle, Male

SINGLETARY, Britain, - He is on the "Petite" Jury list.- *Jury Lists, 1720, Acts #422, [at South Carolina Archives],* pg. 11.

Singletary, Britain, Male

SINGLETARY, Jonathn, - He is on the "Petite" Jury list.- *Jury Lists, 1720, Acts #422, [at South Carolina Archives],* pg. 12.

Singletary, Jonathn, Male

SINGLETARY, Richd, - He is on the "Petite" Jury list.- *Jury Lists, 1720, Acts #422, [at South Carolina Archives],* pg. 12.

Singletary, Richd, Male

SINKLER, Robt, - He is on the "Petite" Jury list.- *Jury Lists, 1720, Acts #422, [at South Carolina Archives],* pg. 13.

Sinkler, Robt, Male

SKEENE, Alexr, Esqr, - He is on the "Petite" Jury list.- *Jury Lists, 1720, Acts #422, [at South Carolina Archives],* pg. 7.

Skeene, Alexr, Esqr, Male

SKREEN, Jona, - He is on the "Petite" Jury list.- *Jury Lists, 1720, Acts #422, [at South Carolina Archives],* pg. 13.

Skreen, Jona, Male

SMALL, Samle, - He is on the "Petite" Jury list.- *Jury Lists, 1720, Acts #422, [at South Carolina Archives]*, pg. 11.

Small, Samle, Male

SMILEY, Jno, - He is on the "Petite" Jury list.- *Jury Lists, 1720, Acts #422, [at South Carolina Archives]*, pg. 5.

Smiley, Jno, Male

SMITH, Christopher, - He is on the "Petite" Jury list.- *Jury Lists, 1720, Acts #422, [at South Carolina Archives]*, pg. 3.

Smith, Christopher, Male

SMITH, Geo, - He is on the "Petite" Jury list.- *Jury Lists, 1720, Acts #422, [at South Carolina Archives]*, pg. 14.

Smith, Geo, Male

SMITH, Geo, - He is on the Grand Jury list.- *Jury Lists, 1720, Acts #422, [at South Carolina Archives]*, pg. 3.

Smith, Geo, Male

SMITH, Geo, - He is on the "Petite" Jury list.- *Jury Lists, 1720, Acts #422, [at South Carolina Archives]*, pg. 12.

Smith, Geo, Male

SMITH, Jno, - He is on the "Petite" Jury list.- *Jury Lists, 1720, Acts #422, [at South Carolina Archives]*, pg. 14.

Smith, Jno, Male

SMITH, Jno, - He is on the "Petite" Jury list.- *Jury Lists, 1720, Acts #422, [at South Carolina Archives]*, pg. 4.

Smith, Jno, Male

SMITH, Jos, - He is on the "Petite" Jury list.- *Jury Lists, 1720, Acts #422, [at South Carolina Archives]*, pg. 8.

Smith, Jos, Male

SMITH, Richd, - He is on the Grand Jury list.- *Jury Lists, 1720, Acts #422, [at South Carolina Archives]*, pg. 3.

Smith, Richd, Male

SMITH, Richd, - He is on the "Petite" Jury list.- *Jury Lists, 1720, Acts #422, [at South Carolina Archives]*, pg. 12.

Smith, Richd, Male

SMITH, Thos, Lieut Colo, - He is on the Grand Jury list.- *Jury Lists, 1720, Acts #422, [at South Carolina Archives]*, pg. 2.

Smith, Thos, Lieut Colo, Male

SMITH, Thos, Lieut Colo, - He is on the "Petite" Jury list.- *Jury Lists, 1720, Acts #422, [at South Carolina Archives]*, pg. 9.

Smith, Thos, Lieut Colo, Male

SMITH, Wm, Ensign, - He is on the Grand Jury list.- *Jury Lists, 1720, Acts #422, [at South Carolina Archives]*, pg. 2.

Smith, Wm, Ensign, Male

SMITH, Wm, Ensigne, - He is on the "Petite" Jury list.- *Jury Lists, 1720, Acts #422, [at South Carolina Archives]*, pg. 9.

Smith, Wm, Ensigne, Male

SNOW, Thos, - He is on the "Petite" Jury list.- *Jury Lists, 1720, Acts #422, [at South Carolina Archives]*, pg. 8.

Snow, Thos, Male

SPENCER, Alexr, - He is on the "Petite" Jury list.- *Jury Lists, 1720, Acts #422, [at South Carolina Archives]*, pg. 6.

Spencer, Alexr, Male

SPENSOR, Wm, - He is on the "Petite" Jury list.- *Jury Lists, 1720, Acts #422, [at South Carolina Archives]*, pg. 6.

Spensor, Wm, Male

SPINCER, Josph, - He is on the "Petite" Jury list.- *Jury Lists, 1720, Acts #422, [at South Carolina Archives]*, pg. 13.

Spincer, Josph, Male

SPLATT, Richd, - He is on the Grand Jury list.- *Jury Lists, 1720, Acts #422, [at South Carolina Archives]*, pg. 2.

Splatt, Richd, Male

SPLATT, Richd, - He is on the "Petite" Jury list.- *Jury Lists, 1720, Acts #422, [at South Carolina Archives]*, pg. 9.

Splatt, Richd, Male

SPRY, Royal, - He is on the "Petite" Jury list.- *Jury Lists, 1720, Acts #422, [at South Carolina Archives]*, pg. 4.

Spry, Royal, Male

ST JULIAN, Jams, - He is on the "Petite" Jury list.- *Jury Lists, 1720, Acts #422, [at South Carolina Archives]*, pg. 9.

St Julian, Jams, Male

ST MARTINE, Jno, - He is on the "Petite" Jury list.- *Jury Lists, 1720, Acts #422, [at South Carolina Archives]*, pg. 12.

St Martine, Jno, Male

STANYARN, Jno, - He is on the "Petite" Jury list.- *Jury Lists, 1720, Acts #422, [at South Carolina Archives]*, pg. 3.

Stanyarn, Jno, Male
STANYARN, Jno, - He is on the Grand Jury list.- *Jury Lists, 1720, Acts #422, [at South Carolina Archives],* pg. 1.
Stanyarn, Jno, Male
STEPHENS, Robt, - He is on the "Petite" Jury list.- *Jury Lists, 1720, Acts #422, [at South Carolina Archives],* pg. 4.
Stephens, Robt, Male
STEWARD, Wm, - He is on the "Petite" Jury list.- *Jury Lists, 1720, Acts #422, [at South Carolina Archives],* pg. 8.
Steward, Wm, Male
STEWART, Jno, - He is on the "Petite" Jury list.- *Jury Lists, 1720, Acts #422, [at South Carolina Archives],* pg. 12.
Stewart, Jno, Male
STOCKS, Jno, - He is on the "Petite" Jury list.- *Jury Lists, 1720, Acts #422, [at South Carolina Archives],* pg. 6.
Stocks, Jno, Male
STOCKS, Jonathan, - He is on the "Petite" Jury list.- *Jury Lists, 1720, Acts #422, [at South Carolina Archives],* pg. 4.
Stocks, Jonathan, Male
STON?, Daniel, - He is on the "Petite" Jury list.- *Jury Lists, 1720, Acts #422, [at South Carolina Archives],* pg. 6.
Ston?, Daniel, Male
STONE, Jno, - He is on the "Petite" Jury list.- *Jury Lists, 1720, Acts #422, [at South Carolina Archives],* pg. 8.
Stone, Jno, Male
STONE, Jno, Junr, - He is on the "Petite" Jury list.- *Jury Lists, 1720, Acts #422, [at South Carolina Archives],* pg. 11.
Stone, Jno, Junr, Male
STONE, Jno, Senr, - He is on the "Petite" Jury list.- *Jury Lists, 1720, Acts #422, [at South Carolina Archives],* pg. 12.
Stone, Jno, Senr, Male
STONE, Josph, - He is on the "Petite" Jury list.- *Jury Lists, 1720, Acts #422, [at South Carolina Archives],* pg. 11.
Stone, Josph, Male
STORY, Rowland, - He is on the "Petite" Jury list.- *Jury Lists, 1720, Acts #422, [at South Carolina Archives],* pg. 6.
Story, Rowland, Male

STOUTENBER, Lucas, Lieut, - He is on the "Petite" Jury list.- *Jury Lists, 1720, Acts #422, [at South Carolina Archives],* pg. 9.
Stoutenber, Lucas, Lieut, Male
STOUTENBER, Lucas, Lieut, - He is on the Grand Jury list.- *Jury Lists, 1720, Acts #422, [at South Carolina Archives],* pg. 2.
Stoutenber, Lucas, Lieut, Male
STRAND, Jno, - He is on the "Petite" Jury list.- *Jury Lists, 1720, Acts #422, [at South Carolina Archives],* pg. 11.
Strand, Jno, Male
STREET, Wm, - He is on the "Petite" Jury list.- *Jury Lists, 1720, Acts #422, [at South Carolina Archives],* pg. 6.
Street, Wm, Male
STURT, Thos, - He is on the "Petite" Jury list.- *Jury Lists, 1720, Acts #422, [at South Carolina Archives],* pg. 9.
Sturt, Thos, Male
SULLIVANE, Corns, - He is on the "Petite" Jury list.- *Jury Lists, 1720, Acts #422, [at South Carolina Archives],* pg. 4.
Sullivane, Corns, Male
SUMERS, Thos, - He is on the "Petite" Jury list.- *Jury Lists, 1720, Acts #422, [at South Carolina Archives],* pg. 11.
Sumers, Thos, Male
SUMMER, Jno, - He is on the "Petite" Jury list.- *Jury Lists, 1720, Acts #422, [at South Carolina Archives],* pg. 12.
Summer, Jno, Male
SUMNER, Benja, - He is on the "Petite" Jury list.- *Jury Lists, 1720, Acts #422, [at South Carolina Archives],* pg. 7.
Sumner, Benja, Male
SUMNER, Nathle, - He is on the "Petite" Jury list.- *Jury Lists, 1720, Acts #422, [at South Carolina Archives],* pg. 8.
Sumner, Nathle, Male
SUMNER, Samle, - He is on the "Petite" Jury list.- *Jury Lists, 1720, Acts #422, [at South Carolina Archives],* pg. 8.
Sumner, Samle, Male
SUTTON, Robt, - He is on the "Petite" Jury list.- *Jury Lists, 1720, Acts #422, [at South Carolina Archives],* pg. 13.
Sutton, Robt, Male
TAGGART, Jams, - He is on the "Petite" Jury list.- *Jury Lists, 1720, Acts #422, [at South Carolina Archives],* pg. 12.

Taggart, Jams, Male

TAVEROON, Stepn, - He is on the "Petite" Jury list.- *Jury Lists, 1720, Acts #422, [at South Carolina Archives]*, pg. 14.

Taveroon, Stepn, Male

TAYLOR, Robt, - He is on the "Petite" Jury list.- *Jury Lists, 1720, Acts #422, [at South Carolina Archives]*, pg. 10.

Taylor, Robt, Male

THOMAS, Edwd, - He is on the "Petite" Jury list.- *Jury Lists, 1720, Acts #422, [at South Carolina Archives]*, pg. 10.

Thomas, Edwd, Male

THOMPSON, ?, - He is on the "Petite" Jury list.- *Jury Lists, 1720, Acts #422, [at South Carolina Archives]*, pg. 13.

Thompson, ?, Male, "Docterr"

TOOMER, Henry, - He is on the "Petite" Jury list.- *Jury Lists, 1720, Acts #422, [at South Carolina Archives]*, pg. 6.

Toomer, Henry, Male

TOOMER, Henry, - He is on the Grand Jury list.- *Jury Lists, 1720, Acts #422, [at South Carolina Archives]*, pg. 1.

Toomer, Henry, Male

TOWNSEN, Thos, - He is on the "Petite" Jury list.- *Jury Lists, 1720, Acts #422, [at South Carolina Archives]*, pg. 4.

Townsen, Thos, Male

TOWNSEND, Danle, - He is on the "Petite" Jury list.- *Jury Lists, 1720, Acts #422, [at South Carolina Archives]*, pg. 9.

Townsend, Danle, Male

TRADD, Robt, - He is on the "Petite" Jury list.- *Jury Lists, 1720, Acts #422, [at South Carolina Archives]*, pg. 8.

Tradd, Robt, Male

TRADD, Robt, - He is on the Grand Jury list.- *Jury Lists, 1720, Acts #422, [at South Carolina Archives]*, pg. 2.

Tradd, Robt, Male

TRESVANT, Isaac, - He is on the "Petite" Jury list.- *Jury Lists, 1720, Acts #422, [at South Carolina Archives]*, pg. 11.

Tresvant, Isaac, Male

TRESVANT, Theor, - He is on the "Petite" Jury list.- *Jury Lists, 1720, Acts #422, [at South Carolina Archives]*, pg. 11.

Tresvant, Theor, Male

TUCKER, Arthur, - He is on the "Petite" Jury list.- *Jury Lists, 1720, Acts #422, [at South Carolina Archives]*, pg. 6.

Tucker, Arthur, Male

TUCKER, Jno, - He is on the "Petite" Jury list.- *Jury Lists, 1720, Acts #422, [at South Carolina Archives]*, pg. 4.

Tucker, Jno, Male

UNDERWOOD, Samle, - He is on the "Petite" Jury list.- *Jury Lists, 1720, Acts #422, [at South Carolina Archives]*, pg. 4.

Underwood, Samle, Male

UPHAM, Thos, Senr, - He is on the "Petite" Jury list.- *Jury Lists, 1720, Acts #422, [at South Carolina Archives]*, pg. 4.

Upham, Thos, Senr, Male

URIN, Robt, - He is on the "Petite" Jury list.- *Jury Lists, 1720, Acts #422, [at South Carolina Archives]*, pg. 4.

Urin, Robt, Male

VANDERHORST, Jno, - He is on the Grand Jury list.- *Jury Lists, 1720, Acts #422, [at South Carolina Archives]*, pg. 3.

Vanderhorst, Jno, Male

VANDERHORST, Jno, - He is on the "Petite" Jury list.- *Jury Lists, 1720, Acts #422, [at South Carolina Archives]*, pg. 12.

Vanderhorst, Jno, Male

VANDERSHOST, Jno, - He is on the Grand Jury list.- *Jury Lists, 1720, Acts #422, [at South Carolina Archives]*, pg. 2.

Vandershost, Jno, Male

VANVELLSEY, Garrett, - He is on the "Petite" Jury list.- *Jury Lists, 1720, Acts #422, [at South Carolina Archives]*, pg. 9.

Vanvellsey, Garrett, Male

VANVELSEN, Edwd, - He is on the "Petite" Jury list.- *Jury Lists, 1720, Acts #422, [at South Carolina Archives]*, pg. 8.

Vanvelsen, Edwd, Male

VANVELSIN?, Garret, - He is on the Grand Jury list.- *Jury Lists, 1720, Acts #422, [at South Carolina Archives]*, pg. 2.

Vanvelsin?, Garret, Male

VARDILE, Antho, - He is on the "Petite" Jury list.- *Jury Lists, 1720, Acts #422, [at South Carolina Archives]*, pg. 12.

Vardile, Antho, Male

VICARIDGE, Jno, - He is on the "Petite" Jury list.- *Jury Lists, 1720, Acts #422, [at South Carolina Archives]*, pg. 9.

Vicaridge, Jno, Male

VIDEAU, Henry Joseph, - He is on the "Petite" Jury list.- *Jury Lists, 1720, Acts #422, [at South Carolina Archives],* pg. 11.

Videau, Henry Joseph, Male

VILLEPONTOIX, Petr, - He is on the "Petite" Jury list.- *Jury Lists, 1720, Acts #422, [at South Carolina Archives],* pg. 10.

Villepontoix, Petr, Male

VINCENT, Geo, - He is on the "Petite" Jury list.- *Jury Lists, 1720, Acts #422, [at South Carolina Archives],* pg. 5.

Vincent, Geo, Male

WAITE, Isaac, - He is on the "Petite" Jury list.- *Jury Lists, 1720, Acts #422, [at South Carolina Archives],* pg. 3.

Waite, Isaac, Male

WALCOTT, Ebinezer, - He is on the "Petite" Jury list.- *Jury Lists, 1720, Acts #422, [at South Carolina Archives],* pg. 4.

Walcott, Ebinezer, Male

WALCOTT, Nathle, - He is on the "Petite" Jury list.- *Jury Lists, 1720, Acts #422, [at South Carolina Archives],* pg. 4.

Walcott, Nathle, Male

WALIS, Wm, - He is on the Grand Jury list.- *Jury Lists, 1720, Acts #422, [at South Carolina Archives],* pg. 3.

Walis, Wm, Male

WALKER, Henry, - He is on the "Petite" Jury list.- *Jury Lists, 1720, Acts #422, [at South Carolina Archives],* pg. 4.

Walker, Henry, Male

WALLACE, Wm, - He is on the "Petite" Jury list.- *Jury Lists, 1720, Acts #422, [at South Carolina Archives],* pg. 7.

Wallace, Wm, Male

WALLACE, Wm, - He is on the Grand Jury list.- *Jury Lists, 1720, Acts #422, [at South Carolina Archives],* pg. 2.

Wallace, Wm, Male

WALTERS, Josph, - He is on the "Petite" Jury list.- *Jury Lists, 1720, Acts #422, [at South Carolina Archives],* pg. 12.

Walters, Josph, Male

WARING, Benj, Capt, - He is on the "Petite" Jury list.- *Jury Lists, 1720, Acts #422, [at South Carolina Archives],* pg. 7.

Waring, Benj, Capt, Male

WARING, Benja, Capt, - He is on the Grand Jury list.- *Jury Lists, 1720, Acts #422, [at South Carolina Archives],* pg. 2.

Waring, Benja, Capt, Male

WARING, Richd, - He is on the "Petite" Jury list.- *Jury Lists, 1720, Acts #422, [at South Carolina Archives],* pg. 8.

Waring, Richd, Male

WARING, Thos, ?, - He is on the Grand Jury list.- *Jury Lists, 1720, Acts #422, [at South Carolina Archives],* pg. 2.

Waring, Thos, ?, Male

WARING, Thos, ?, - He is on the "Petite" Jury list.- *Jury Lists, 1720, Acts #422, [at South Carolina Archives],* pg. 7.

Waring, Thos, ?, Male

WARNOCK, Abra, Senr, - He is on the "Petite" Jury list.- *Jury Lists, 1720, Acts #422, [at South Carolina Archives],* pg. 12.

Warnock, Abra, Senr, Male

WARNOCK, Andw, - He is on the "Petite" Jury list.- *Jury Lists, 1720, Acts #422, [at South Carolina Archives],* pg. 11.

Warnock, Andw, Male

WATSON, Wm, - He is on the "Petite" Jury list.- *Jury Lists, 1720, Acts #422, [at South Carolina Archives],* pg. 12.

Watson, Wm, Male

WATTS, Wm, - He is on the "Petite" Jury list.- *Jury Lists, 1720, Acts #422, [at South Carolina Archives],* pg. 13.

Watts, Wm, Male

WAY, Aaron, Senr, - He is on the "Petite" Jury list.- *Jury Lists, 1720, Acts #422, [at South Carolina Archives],* pg. 7.

Way, Aaron, Senr, Male

WAY, Ebenezer, - He is on the "Petite" Jury list.- *Jury Lists, 1720, Acts #422, [at South Carolina Archives],* pg. 7.

Way, Ebenezer, Male

WAY, Moses, - He is on the "Petite" Jury list.- *Jury Lists, 1720, Acts #422, [at South Carolina Archives],* pg. 8.

Way, Moses, Male

WEASTCOAT, Jno, - He is on the "Petite" Jury list.- *Jury Lists, 1720, Acts #422, [at South Carolina Archives],* pg. 12.

Weastcoat, Jno, Male

WEATHERLY, Thos, - He is on the "Petite" Jury list.- *Jury Lists, 1720, Acts #422, [at South Carolina Archives],* pg. 6.

Weatherly, Thos, Male
WEAVERLY, Thos, Lieut, - He is on the "Petite" Jury list.- *Jury Lists, 1720, Acts #422, [at South Carolina Archives]*, pg. 3.
Weaverly, Thos, Lieut, Male
WEBB, Benja, - He is on the "Petite" Jury list.- *Jury Lists, 1720, Acts #422, [at South Carolina Archives]*, pg. 13.
Webb, Benja, Male
WEBB, Thos, - He is on the "Petite" Jury list.- *Jury Lists, 1720, Acts #422, [at South Carolina Archives]*, pg. 12.
Webb, Thos, Male
WEEKLEY, Edwd, - He is on the "Petite" Jury list.- *Jury Lists, 1720, Acts #422, [at South Carolina Archives]*, pg. 7.
Weekley, Edwd, Male
WEEKLEY, Edwd, - He is on the Grand Jury list.- *Jury Lists, 1720, Acts #422, [at South Carolina Archives]*, pg. 2.
Weekley, Edwd, Male
WELLS, Edgar, - He is on the "Petite" Jury list.- *Jury Lists, 1720, Acts #422, [at South Carolina Archives]*, pg. 11.
Wells, Edgar, Male
WELLS, Syleas, - He is on the "Petite" Jury list.- *Jury Lists, 1720, Acts #422, [at South Carolina Archives]*, pg. 6.
Wells, Syleas, Male
WELLS, Wm, - He is on the "Petite" Jury list.- *Jury Lists, 1720, Acts #422, [at South Carolina Archives]*, pg. 8.
Wells, Wm, Male
WESBURY, Thos, - He is on the "Petite" Jury list.- *Jury Lists, 1720, Acts #422, [at South Carolina Archives]*, pg. 6.
Wesbury, Thos, Male
WEST, Samle, - He is on the Grand Jury list.- *Jury Lists, 1720, Acts #422, [at South Carolina Archives]*, pg. 2.
West, Samle, Male
WEST, Samle, - He is on the "Petite" Jury list.- *Jury Lists, 1720, Acts #422, [at South Carolina Archives]*, pg. 7.
West, Samle, Male
WESTBURY, Wm, - He is on the "Petite" Jury list.- *Jury Lists, 1720, Acts #422, [at South Carolina Archives]*, pg. 5.
Westbury, Wm, Male

WHEALDING, Jona, - He is on the "Petite" Jury list.- *Jury Lists, 1720, Acts #422, [at South Carolina Archives]*, pg. 12.
Whealding, Jona, Male
WHITE, Antho, - He is on the "Petite" Jury list.- *Jury Lists, 1720, Acts #422, [at South Carolina Archives]*, pg. 12.
White, Antho, Male
WHITE, Jno, - He is on the "Petite" Jury list.- *Jury Lists, 1720, Acts #422, [at South Carolina Archives]*, pg. 13.
White, Jno, Male
WHITE, Nathle, - He is on the "Petite" Jury list.- *Jury Lists, 1720, Acts #422, [at South Carolina Archives]*, pg. 8.
White, Nathle, Male
WHITMASH, Jno, - He is on the "Petite" Jury list.- *Jury Lists, 1720, Acts #422, [at South Carolina Archives]*, pg. 5.
Whitmash, Jno, Male
WIGFALL, Samle, Senr, - He is on the "Petite" Jury list.- *Jury Lists, 1720, Acts #422, [at South Carolina Archives]*, pg. 13.
Wigfall, Samle, Senr, Male
WIGG, Richd, - He is on the "Petite" Jury list.- *Jury Lists, 1720, Acts #422, [at South Carolina Archives]*, pg. 5.
Wigg, Richd, Male
WIGG, Richd, - He is on the Grand Jury list.- *Jury Lists, 1720, Acts #422, [at South Carolina Archives]*, pg. 3.
Wigg, Richd, Male
WILKINS, Jno, - He is on the "Petite" Jury list.- *Jury Lists, 1720, Acts #422, [at South Carolina Archives]*, pg. 6.
Wilkins, Jno, Male
WILKINS, Jno, - He is on the Grand Jury list.- *Jury Lists, 1720, Acts #422, [at South Carolina Archives]*, pg. 1.
Wilkins, Jno, Male
WILKINS, Wm, - He is on the Grand Jury list.- *Jury Lists, 1720, Acts #422, [at South Carolina Archives]*, pg. 1.
Wilkins, Wm, Male
WILKINS, Wm, - He is on the "Petite" Jury list.- *Jury Lists, 1720, Acts #422, [at South Carolina Archives]*, pg. 6.
Wilkins, Wm, Male
WILKINSON, Christopher, - He is on the "Petite" Jury list.- *Jury Lists, 1720, Acts #422, [at South Carolina Archives]*, pg. 4.

Wilkinson, Christopher, Male
WILKINSON, Christopher, - He is on the Grand Jury list.- *Jury Lists, 1720, Acts #422, [at South Carolina Archives]*, pg. 1.
Wilkinson, Christopher, Male
WILKINSON, Robt, - He is on the "Petite" Jury list.- *Jury Lists, 1720, Acts #422, [at South Carolina Archives]*, pg. 5.
Wilkinson, Robt, Male
WILLER, Jno, - He is on the Grand Jury list.- *Jury Lists, 1720, Acts #422, [at South Carolina Archives]*, pg. 1.
Willer, Jno, Male
WILLIAMS, Jno, ?, - He is on the Grand Jury list.- *Jury Lists, 1720, Acts #422, [at South Carolina Archives]*, pg. 2.
Williams, Jno, ?, Male
WILLIAMS, John, ?, - He is on the "Petite" Jury list.- *Jury Lists, 1720, Acts #422, [at South Carolina Archives]*, pg. 7.
Williams, John, ?, Male
WILLIAMS, Wm, - He is on the "Petite" Jury list.- *Jury Lists, 1720, Acts #422, [at South Carolina Archives]*, pg. 4.
Williams, Wm, Male
WILLIAMSON, Jno, - He is on the "Petite" Jury list.- *Jury Lists, 1720, Acts #422, [at South Carolina Archives]*, pg. 3.
Williamson, Jno, Male
WILTER, Jno, - He is on the "Petite" Jury list.- *Jury Lists, 1720, Acts #422, [at South Carolina Archives]*, pg. 6.
Wilter, Jno, Male
WINBURN, Thos, - He is on the "Petite" Jury list.- *Jury Lists, 1720, Acts #422, [at South Carolina Archives]*, pg. 5.
Winburn, Thos, Male
WOOD, Henry, - He is on the "Petite" Jury list.- *Jury Lists, 1720, Acts #422, [at South Carolina Archives]*, pg. 6.

Wood, Henry, Male
WOOD, Robt, - He is on the "Petite" Jury list.- *Jury Lists, 1720, Acts #422, [at South Carolina Archives]*, pg. 6.
Wood, Robt, Male
WOODWARD, Jno, - He is on the Grand Jury list.- *Jury Lists, 1720, Acts #422, [at South Carolina Archives]*, pg. 2.
Woodward, Jno, Male
WOODWARD, Jno, - He is on the "Petite" Jury list.- *Jury Lists, 1720, Acts #422, [at South Carolina Archives]*, pg. 7.
Woodward, Jno, Male
WOODWARD, Richd, - He is on the "Petite" Jury list.- *Jury Lists, 1720, Acts #422, [at South Carolina Archives]*, pg. 6.
Woodward, Richd, Male
WRAGG, Josph, - He is on the Grand Jury list.- *Jury Lists, 1720, Acts #422, [at South Carolina Archives]*, pg. 1.
Wragg, Josph, Male
WRAGG, Josph, - He is on the "Petite" Jury list.- *Jury Lists, 1720, Acts #422, [at South Carolina Archives]*, pg. 9.
Wragg, Josph, Male
WUXHAM, Jams, - He is on the "Petite" Jury list.- *Jury Lists, 1720, Acts #422, [at South Carolina Archives]*, pg. 5.
Wuxham, Jams, Male
WYAT, Stephen, - He is on the "Petite" Jury list.- *Jury Lists, 1720, Acts #422, [at South Carolina Archives]*, pg. 14.
Wyat, Stephen, Male
YARMAN, Petr, - He is on the "Petite" Jury list.- *Jury Lists, 1720, Acts #422, [at South Carolina Archives]*, pg. 10.
Yarman, Petr, Male

STEMMONS PUBLISHING, 1078 Shields Lane, South Jordan, Utah 84095, 801-254-2152 (Call between 9:00 a.m. and 5:00 p.m. Monday through Friday. If no one answers, please leave a message.), stemmonspublishing@gmail.com

The importance of census records and other population lists cannot be overstated in terms of the help they are in locating people in a specific area. This allows one to examine other records in that area. This is one of our main goals and why we do business. What we are trying to accomplish is a work in progress. We hope to improve as we go along. Thank you for your patience.

Petitions are an important example of these population lists.

Thank you for the opportunity to serve you.

Sincerely,
John Stemmons

A LIST OF OUR GENEALOGY BOOKS

AL-01 **ALABAMA 1800 PETITIONERS [-1804]**© Compiled by John D Stemmons, 2021. This book compiled from *Territorial Papers of the United States* contains 253 entries for a very early period in Alabama's history. It may contain some biographical details and clues to prior residence. It can help substitute for the missing federal census. For information on how to obtain this book search by the title or "Books by John Stemmons" at Amazon.com. This comes automatically with a paperback binding. It includes but is not limited to petitions regarding:
- Seeking new territory due to the rapid migration from Georgia, etc.
- Petition seeking confirmation of land grants obtained from other governments.

36 Pages $7.20

AL-02 **ALABAMA 1810 PETITIONERS, ETC., [1805-1814]**© Compiled by John D Stemmons, 2021. This book compiled from *Territorial Papers of the United States* contains 1687 entries for a very early period in Alabama's history. It includes a census of Madison County, taken Jan 1809. It may contain some biographical details and clues to prior residence. It can help substitute for the missing federal census. For information on how to obtain this book search by the title or "Books by John Stemmons" at Amazon.com. This comes automatically with a paperback binding. It includes but is not limited to petitions regarding:
- Issues relating to land.
- Petition of inhabitants east of Pearl River seeking to form a new territory.
- 1809 census of Madison County.
- Inhabitants of Tombigbee seeking for their purchases from the Spanish to be duty free at "Fort Stoddart".

176 Pages $35.20

AL-03 **ALABAMA 1820 PETITIONERS, ETC., [1815-1824]**© Compiled by John D Stemmons, 2021. This book compiled from *Territorial Papers of the United States* contains 3913 entries for a fast-growing period in Alabama's history. It may contain some biographical details and clues to prior residence. It can help substitute for the missing federal census. For information on how to obtain this book search by the title or "Books by John Stemmons" at Amazon.com. This comes automatically with a paperback binding. It includes but is not limited to petitions regarding:
- Merchants and traders of St. Stephens seeking to establish that town as a port of delivery.
- Inhabitants of eastern part of MS territory, who lost much income/property in the wars with England & Indians.
- Inhabitants of Alabama Territory opposing the "settlements on the western side of the Mobile & Tombigby rivers" being made part of Mississippi.
- List of Letters, 9 Jan 1819, remaining in Huntsville Post Office.
- Issues about military and local officers.
- Memorial, ref. 20 Jan 1817, to Congress from inhabitants of Mobile complaining that Ft Charlotte is indefensible.

407 Pages $81.40

AR-01 **ARKANSAS PETITIONERS, ETC. 1800, 1810 [1795-1814]**© Compiled by John D Stemmons, 2021. This book compiled from *Territorial Papers of the United States* contains 261 entries and is a partial replacement for the missing federal censuses of 1800 and 1810. As a result, it is a very helpful resource in establishing residence of people in Arkansas during that early formative period in the state's history. These people include some of earliest you will find that established the foundation of what was to become the great state that Arkansas now is. This also makes it possible to determine what other records might be available for further research. Some additional biographical details may be included, and possible relationships with others may be revealed. For information on how to obtain this book search by the title or "Books by John Stemmons" at Amazon.com. This comes automatically with a paperback binding. It includes but is not limited to petitions regarding:
- Issues relating to land.
- Inhabitants of Arkansas District expressing concern about the hostile attitude of the Cherokees nearby.
- Issues about military and local officers.

43 Pages $8.60

AR-02 **ARKANSAS PETITIONERS, ETC. 1820 [1815-1824]**© Compiled by John D Stemmons, 2021. This book compiled from *Territorial Papers of the United States* contains 1936 entries and is a partial replacement for the missing federal census of 1820. As a result, it is a very helpful resource in establishing residence of people in Arkansas during that fast-growing territorial period prior to becoming a state. Unfortunately, the 1820 census is not available to help track these people. That is why this new book can help. It is even better in some respects than the census because it helps us understand some of the challenges they faced. It also makes possible the determination of other records that might be available for further research. Some additional biographical details may be included, and possible relationships with others may be revealed. Even the names of some Native Americans are included as well as a few potential residents of Oklahoma. For information on how to obtain this book search by the title or "Books by John Stemmons" at Amazon.com. This comes automatically with a paperback binding. It includes but is not limited to petitions regarding:
- Issues relating to land.
- Issues relating to Native Americans.
- Citizens of Arkansas County describing the good location of the Town of Arkansas.
- Appointments about military and local officers, etc.
- Inhabitants of Arkansas and Phillips Counties seeking a mail route from the Town of Arkansas to the "Post of Ouachita in Louisianna."
- Abstract of Grand and Petit Jurors, Oct term, 1824 listing compensation for their attendance at a Superior Court held at Little Rock.

216 Pages $43.20

1001-**GEORGIA PETITIONS 1778-1784**© Compiled by John D Stemmons, 2004. This book contains 256 entries for a very early period in Georgia's history. For information on how to obtain this book search by the title or "Books by John Stemmons" at

Amazon.com. This comes automatically with a paperback binding. It includes but is not limited to petitions regarding:

- A desire for a new district.
- A request for local courts.
- Issues about military and local officers.
- Request for protection against enemies.
- A request for pardon, amnesty, etc.
- Description of hardship.

44 pages $8.80

1002-GEORGIA PETITIONS 1785-1794© Compiled by John D Stemmons, 2004. Contains 3720 entries which includes about 25% of the heads of household in Georgia at that time. As such this publication is an excellent substitute for the missing Georgia 1790 federal census. It even includes many names for Burke and Washington Counties which suffered severe record loss in the early years. For information on how to obtain this book search by the title or "Books by John Stemmons" at Amazon.com. This comes automatically with a paperback binding. It includes but is not limited to petitions regarding:

- Issues regarding local agencies, boundary changes, etc.
- Issues regarding religion and churches.
- Issues about military and local officers.
- Asking for measures to control slaves.
- Recommendation for a business opportunity.
- Seeking resolution of land problems, land fraud, etc.
- Asking for increased tobacco inspection fees.
- Request for protection against Indians.
- Issues about crimes, pardon, amnesty, etc.
- Description of hardship.

367 pages $73.40

IL-01 ILLINOIS PETITIONS, ETC., 1760-1810 [1755-1814]© Compiled by John D Stemmons, 2021, this book contains 3680 names from *The Territorial Papers of the U.S.* This covers a period of time even before the federal census of 1790. And while no federal censuses exists for Illinois from 1790-1810, these records nicely substitute for those missing documents. It should be noted that 1004-**A PARTIAL CENSUS FOR INDIANA TERRITORY 1810** includes most if not all the names for 1810. A study to determine that they were the same was inconclusive and so, just in the outside chance there might be some that were not the same, it was felt that they should be included. The convenience of having them together outweighs their exclusion. These records include an incredible amount of information about these early people. One can see the change from a mostly French culture to that of English. The transition was not always peaceful. Included are census records, lists of inhabitants, and much more. While the federal censuses are missing that would help track these people, these records are even better in some respects than the census because it helps us understand some of the challenges they faced. That is why this new book can help. Some additional biographical details may be included, plus possible relationships with other family members. For information on how to obtain this book search by the title or "Books by John Stemmons" at Amazon.com. This comes automatically with a paperback binding. It includes but is not limited to petitions regarding:

- Issues relating to land.
- Issues relating to Native Americans.
- List of inhabitants at Kaskaskias before 1783.
- Appointments about military and local officers, etc.
- Lands claimed and possessed by inhabitants of the District of Cahokia on or before 1783 that still existed after 29 May 1790.
- Applications for lands in the District of Cahokia by persons claiming as settlers under the state of Virginia, if the settlements were made on or before 1783 that still existed after 29 May 1790.
- List of families at the Prairie du Pont, undated, but enclosed in St. Clair's report 10 Feb 1791.

349 Pages $69.80

IN-01 THE TERRITORY NORTHWEST OF THE RIVER OHIO, PETITIONERS, ETC., 1790-1800 [1785-1804] (Present day Indiana)© Compiled by John D Stemmons, 2021. This book was compiled from *Territorial Papers of the United States.* 1790 contains 242 names found on petitions, etc., including a census of heads of household for Vincennes. 1800 only includes 76 names and so is not as valuable as 1790. The population of Indiana would have increased significantly between 1790 and 1800. This is still a very early time prior to Indiana becoming a state. Unfortunately, there is no 1790 or 1800 census existing to help track these people. Therefore, we must do what we can with what is available. That is why this new book is so helpful. It is even better in some respects than the census because it helps us understand some of the challenges they faced. It also makes possible the determination of other records that might be available for further research such as land grants. Even the names of some Native Americans are listed. Some additional biographical details may be included, plus possible relationships with other family members. For information on how to obtain this book search by the title or "Books by John Stemmons" at Amazon.com. This comes automatically with a paperback binding. It includes but is not limited to petitions regarding:

- Issues relating to land.
- Heads of families settled at Post Vincennes on or before 1783 and residents at this time [13 Jul 1790] who are entitled to donation lands.
- Issues relating to Native Americans.
- Inhabitants of Vincennes who migrated to Vincennes around 1786 and received land, but never obtained a deed.
- Appointments about military and local officers, etc.

38 Pages $7.60

1003-INDIANA ELECTION RETURNS 1809, 1812© Compiled by John D and E. Diane Stemmons, 2004. This compilation of 3576 entries includes the names found in the territorial election returns which documents are in the Indiana Historical Society. Also included is a poll book of an election for Dearborn County in 1809 as found in *Territorial Papers of the United States.* All entries in this book are also found in *A Partial Census for Indiana Territory 1810.* The book *Indiana Election Returns, 1809, 1812* was compiled for just the election returns simply because they are one entire record source and may have some value in that. For information on how to obtain this book search by the title or "Books by John Stemmons" at Amazon.com. This comes automatically with a paperback binding.

285 pages $57.00

1004-A PARTIAL CENSUS FOR INDIANA TERRITORY 1810© Compiled by John D and E. Diane Stemmons, 2021. With 8602 entries this book includes name lists found in *Territorial Papers of the United States* for Indiana Territory during the period 1805 through 1814. It also provides the names in *Indiana Election Returns 1809, 1812* listed above. Since there were approximately 4300 heads of households in the territory in 1810, *A Partial Census for Indiana Territory 1810* probably lists virtually every head of household in Indiana Territory for the time period. It makes an excellent substitute for the missing federal census for 1810. In addition, it includes names of people living in what is now Illinois, but which was part of Indiana Territory before 1809. Therefore, *A Partial Census for Indiana Territory 1810* is also a partial census of Illinois in the years between 1805 to 1809. For information on how to obtain this book search by the title or "Books by John Stemmons" at Amazon.com. This comes automatically with a paperback binding. It includes but is not limited to petitions regarding:

- Issues relating to land.
- Heads of families settled at Post Vincennes on or before 1783 and residents at this time [13 Jul 1790] who are entitled to donation lands.
- Issues relating to Native Americans.
- Inhabitants of Vincennes who migrated to Vincennes around 1786 and received land, but never obtained a deed.

- Appointments about military and local officers, etc.

574 pages $114.80

KY-01 KENTUCKY 1800, BARREN COUNTY TAX BOOK©

Compiled by John D Stemmons, 2021. It contains 494 names from the Barren County tax list and 1 from *The Territorial Papers of the U.S.* Even though the 1800 census is missing this list it provides an amazing amount of information that substitutes nicely for that missing census, including white and black males aged 16-21 and those 21 and over. This is the kind of information one would expect to find on the census for that period. This list includes all taxable heads of household. Some additional biographical details may be included, plus possible relationships with other family members. The names of the blacks may be found in court, land, and probate records. For information on how to obtain this book search by the title or "Books by John Stemmons" at Amazon.com. This comes automatically with a paperback binding.

65 Pages $13.00

LA-01 ARKANSAS PETITIONS 1800 [1795-1804] and ORLEANS TERRITORY (NOW LOUISIANA) PETITIONS, ETC., 1800 [1795-1804]©

Compiled by John D Stemmons, 2021. This book was compiled from *Territorial Papers of the United States* and contains 495 names for Louisiana and 3 from Arkansas. Since no federal census exists for Arkansas and Louisiana for 1800, these records nicely substitute for those missing documents. These records include an incredible amount of information about these early people. While the federal censuses are missing that would help track these people, these records are even better in some respects than the census because it helps us understand some of the challenges they faced. That is why this new book can help. Some additional biographical details may be included, plus possible relationships with other family members. For information on how to obtain this book search by the title or "Books by John Stemmons" at Amazon.com. This comes automatically with a paperback binding. It includes but is not limited to petitions regarding:

- Inhabitants of Pointe Coupee to Gov. Claiborne, requesting military aid because of fears of a slave revolt.
- Characterization of New Orleans residents, 1 July 1804.
- Address from the free people of color Jan. 1804, volunteering for military service.
- Memorial to Congress from merchants of New Orleans, 9 Jan 1804, offering allegiance to the US.
- Appointments about military and local officers, etc.

47 Pages $9.40

MO-01 MISSOURI PETITIONERS, ETC., 1780-1820 [1775-1824]©

Compiled by John D Stemmons, 2021. This book was compiled from *Territorial Papers of the United States* and contains 1 name for 1780, 12 names for 1790, 19 names for 1800, 5057 names for 1810, and 1509 names for 1820. The later lists begin to approach the number needed to include most heads of household, and nicely substitute for missing or no censuses. These records include an incredible amount of information about these early people. While censuses help track people, the records this book includes are even better in some respects than the census because it helps us understand some of their personal feelings and challenges, they faced. Some additional biographical details may be included, plus possible relationships with other family members. For information on how to obtain this book search by the title or "Books by John Stemmons" at Amazon.com. This comes automatically with a paperback binding. It includes but is not limited to petitions, etc., regarding:

- Resolution recommending distinction between Americans and Frenchmen should be done away.
- Letter from U.S. President to Chief White Hairs and the warriors of the Osages, informing them of the Lewis and Clark expedition, and promising them a resident agent.

- Many petitions, etc., expressing their support and confidence in Governor Wilkinson. He was involved in scandals and controversies.
- Memorial recommending replacements for Governor Wilkinson.
- Petition expressing concern about changing the form of territorial government before they are adequately prepared.
- Memorial concerning the large number of their Spanish land claims that are being rejected.
- Lists of civil and military officers.
- Petition seeking a grant of a township of land for the support of the school as had been done in other areas.
- Petition seeking pre-emption rights for the services given in defending the frontier in Boon's Lick Settlement around 1815.
- Petitions relating to the New Madrid & Little Prairie earthquake.
- Petitions asking for new post offices and routes, etc.

552 pages $110.40

MI-01 MICHIGAN PETITIONS, ETC. 1790-1810 [1785-1814]©

Compiled by John D Stemmons, 2021. This book was compiled from *Territorial Papers of the United States.* It contains 1 name for 1790, 794 names for 1800, and 1335 names for 1810. Clearly, that is not enough for 1790, but the others begin to approach the number needed. Especially is this so for 1810 because we are fortunate enough to have much of what appears to be the federal 1810 census. Since no federal census exists for 1800, these records nicely substitute for those missing documents. These records include an incredible amount of information about these early people. While censuses help track people, the records this book includes are even better in some respects than the census because it helps us understand some of their personal feelings and challenges, they faced. Some additional biographical details may be included, plus possible relationships with other family members. For information on how to obtain this book search by the title or "Books by John Stemmons" at Amazon.com. This comes automatically with a paperback binding. It includes but is not limited to petitions regarding:

- Inhabitants of Detroit seeking new territory because of distance to travel to the headquarters of Indiana Territory.
- Appointments about military and local officers, etc.
- Inhabitants of Wayne County seeking clarification of the status of their land.
- 1810 Census of the District of Detroit.
- Inhabitants of Michigan Ter. seeking time to file claims to their land.
- List, 23 Jul 1812, of patents received from the General Land Office for private claims in the District of Detroit.
- Petition from inhabitants of Michigan Territory asking that the new territorial code be printed also in French.
- Petition to Thomas Jefferson, from inhabitants of Michigan Territory complaining of Governor William Hull and Supreme Court Chief Justice Augustus B. Woodward.

222 Pages $44.40

MS-01 MISSISSIPPI TERRITORIAL PETITIONERS, ETC. 1800 [1795-1804]©

Compiled by John D Stemmons, 2021. This book was compiled from *Territorial Papers of the United States and* contains 2566 names found on petitions, etc., from Mississippi Territory for this time period. This was during a fast-growing era prior to Mississippi becoming a state. Unfortunately, there is no 1800 census existing to help track these people. That is why this new book can help. It is even better in some respects than the census because it helps us understand some of the challenges they faced. It also makes possible the determination of other records that might be available for further research such as Spanish land grants. Some additional biographical details may be included, plus possible relationships with other family members. For information on how to obtain this book search by the title or "Books by John Stemmons" at Amazon.com.

This comes automatically with a paperback binding. It includes but is not limited to petitions regarding:

- Citizens of territory asking land office to be in the area, settlers have pre-emption right, & suffrage be for males of age and US citizens & residents of territory for 6 months.
- Memorial by citizens of the territory, who obtained land before the area became part of the US.
- Testimonials, ca 1802, by individuals regarding the service of John Steele, secretary of the territory.
- Memorial by citizens of the territory seeking that "moderate grants [be] made to actual settlers on unappropriated lands,"
- Merchants of Natchez, complaining of the extra duties they must pay for merchandise shipped from the US.

209 Pages $41.80

MS-02 MISSISSIPPI TERRITORIAL PETITIONS, ETC. 1810 [1805-1814] and WEST FLORIDA 1820 PETITIONERS [1815-1824]© Compiled by John D Stemmons, 2021. This book was compiled from *Territorial Papers of the United States* and contains 1061 names found on petitions, etc., from Mississippi Territory for the period 1810 [1805-1814]. It also includes a list of 76 names on a petition to Congress, 11 Dec 1816, by inhabitants of Jackson County, Mississippi Territory, many of whom settled on land in West Florida while under Spanish control and now seek for their grant to be confirmed by the US. It is being included with Mississippi Territory because it is basically the same time period and place of residence. This was during a fast-growing time prior to Mississippi and Florida becoming states. Unfortunately, there is no 1810 or 1820 census existing to help track these people. That is why this new book can help. It is even better in some respects than the census because it helps us understand some of the challenges they faced. It also makes possible the determination of other records that might be available for further research. Some additional biographical details may be included, and possible relationships with others may be revealed. For information on how to obtain this book search by the title or "Books by John Stemmons" at Amazon.com. This comes automatically with a paperback binding. It includes but is not limited to petitions regarding:

- Inhabitants of the territory seeking adjustment of land claims obtained from the British Government.
- Inhabitants of the territory seek for a road to be built that follows the Pearl River which would shorten the route from Nashville to New Orleans.
- Inhabitants of Amite and Wilkinson Counties seek establishment of a post office.
- Memorial by citizens of the territory (Americans by birth?) seeking a postponement of statehood for the territory.
- Inhabitants of Jackson Co., Mississippi Territory, many of whom settled on land in West Florida while under Spanish control seek for their grant to be confirmed by the US.

108 Pages $21.60

NJ-01-NEW JERSEY PETITIONS 1740, 1745 THROUGH 1754© Compiled by John D Stemmons, 2021. It contains 740 entries for a period of time in New Jersey when records are sparse. While that may not seem like very many names, it was during the time when the population was small, and the residence of people was sometimes hard to track. In looking through these petitions, it appears that the people of this era had basically the same concerns we have. One can see the forces of democracy beginning to stir that were to result in independence from Great Britain just a short three decades away. We can obtain a hint of the personal concerns of these people and what was important to them in this exciting historical time. Even at this time of great distress and hardship life had to go on. These petitions are almost like an open window into the lives of these people. For information on how to obtain this book search by the title or "Books by John Stemmons" at Amazon.com. This comes automatically with a paperback binding. It includes but is not limited to petitions regarding:

- Issues regarding exports and imports.
- Issues regarding devaluation of currency, money supply, etc.
- Issues regarding local agencies, boundary changes, etc.
- Seeking new legislation.
- Issues about military and government officers.
- Seeking resolution of land problems, etc.
- Protesting against the great number of taverns.
- Resolution of tax issues.
- Issues about crimes, pardon, amnesty, etc.

84 pages $16.80

NJ-02-NEW JERSEY PETITIONS 1755-1764© Compiled by John D Stemmons, 2004. Contains 2389 entries from many petitions submitted because of concerns about the French and Indian War. This book is an excellent census substitute. For information on how to obtain this book search by the title or "Books by John Stemmons" at Amazon.com. This comes automatically with a paperback binding. It includes petitions regarding:

- Issues regarding local agencies, boundary changes, etc.
- Issues about roads, bridges, etc.
- Opposition to importing slaves.
- Seeking naturalization.
- Seeking new legislation.
- Issues about military and government affairs.
- Request for reimbursement from the government.
- Request for protection against enemies.
- Seeking resolution of land problems, etc.
- Protesting against dispensing of "spirituous liquors"
- Issues about crimes, pardon, amnesty, etc.
- Description of hardship.

246 pages $49.20

NJ-03-NEW JERSEY PETITIONS 1765-1774© Compiled by John D Stemmons, 2004. This book contains 806 entries. While a small percent of the population, it represents the time leading up to the Revolution. For information on how to obtain this book search by the title or "Books by John Stemmons" at Amazon.com. This comes automatically with a paperback binding. It includes but is not limited to petitions regarding:

- Issues regarding agriculture, exports and imports.
- Request for permission to beg, financial support, etc.
- Issues about religion and churches.
- Request for medical standards.
- Issues regarding devaluation of currency, money supply, etc.
- Issues regarding local agencies, boundary changes, etc.
- Issues on hunting, fishing, etc.
- Issues about roads, bridges, etc.
- Issues relating to slavery.
- Issues about military and government affairs.
- Seeking resolution of land problems, etc.
- Issues about crimes, pardon, amnesty, etc.

99 pages $19.80

NJ-04-NEW JERSEY PETITIONS 1775-1784© Compiled by John D Stemmons, 2005. This book contains 6201 entries which is about 29% of the heads of household living in New Jersey at that time (not counting duplicate names.) It represents the historic period during the Revolution. For information on how to obtain this book search by the title or "Books by John Stemmons" at Amazon.com. This comes automatically with a paperback binding. It includes but is not limited to petitions regarding:

- Issues regarding trade, exports, and imports.
- Issues regarding devaluation of currency, money supply, price controls, etc.
- Issues on religion and churches.

- Issues regarding local agencies, boundary changes or disputes, etc.
- Issues on court cases.
- Request for guardianship of children.
- Issues about roads, bridges, canals, etc.
- Issues on slavery.
- Seeking new legislation or repealing old laws.
- Issues about military and government affairs and officers.
- Issues about payment from the government.
- Issues on independence and the Revolutionary War.
- Request for protection against enemies.
- Seeking resolution of property and land problems, etc.
- Issues about crimes, pardon, amnesty, etc.
- Resolution of tax issues.

559 pages $111.80

NJ-05-NEW JERSEY PETITIONS 1785-1794 Volumes 1-2© Compiled by John D Stemmons, 2005. This book contains 10,353 entries which covers about 35% of the heads of household for that time, not counting duplicate names. For information on how to obtain this book search by the title or "Books by John Stemmons" at Amazon.com. This comes automatically with a paperback binding. It includes but is not limited to petitions regarding:

- Economic issues regarding the devaluation of currency, public debt, etc.
- Issues on religion and churches.
- Issues regarding counties and towns, etc.
- Issues on court cases.
- Issues regarding hunting on private property, fishing, etc.
- Issues about roads, bridges, canals, ferries, etc.
- Issues relating to schools.
- Issues on slavery.
- Seeking new legislation or repealing existing laws.
- Issues about military and government affairs and officers.
- Seeking payment from the government.
- Expressing approval of the U.S. Constitution.
- Seeking resolution of property and land problems, etc.
- Issues about crimes, pardon, amnesty, etc.
- Resolution of tax issues.

Volume 1, A Through K, pages 462 $92.40
Volume 2, L Through Z, pages 470 $94.00

NJ-06 NEW JERSEY PETITIONERS, ETC., 1800 [1795-1804] Volumes 1-3© Compiled by John Stemmons, 2021. All volumes of this book contain 13,144 names. Unlike the tax ratables, these records cover the entire state for the period just after the Revolutionary War These records provide a place of residence which can lead to other records to search. For information on how to obtain this book search by the title or "Books by John Stemmons" at Amazon.com. This comes automatically with a paperback binding. It includes but is not limited to petitions regarding:

- Public buildings including poor house, taverns, banks, etc.
- Issues on religion and churches.
- Issues regarding counties and towns, etc.
- Issues on court cases.
- Concerning voting opportunities
- Issues about roads, bridges, canals, ferries, water rights, storage of gunpowder, etc.
- Issues relating to schools.
- Issues on slavery.
- Seeking new legislation or repealing existing laws.
- Issues about military and government affairs and officers.
- Seeking payment from the government.
- Seeking resolution of property and land problems, etc.
- Issues about crimes, pardon, amnesty, etc.
- Resolution of tax issues.

Volume 1, A Through E, pages 423 $84.60

Volume 2, F Through R, pages 529 $105.80
Volume 3, S Through Z, pages 358 $71.60

NJ-07 NEW JERSEY TAX RATABLES, 1770 [1765-1774] This book contains 2373 names of those who are taxable. They do include important details about the property they held and may provide clues regarding relationship, etc. For information on how to obtain this book search by the title or "Books by John Stemmons" at Amazon.com. This comes automatically with a paperback binding.

250 pages $50.00

NJ-08 NEW JERSEY TAX RATABLES, 1780 [1775-1784] This book contains 4358 names of those who are taxable. It includes important details about the property they held and may provide clues regarding relationship, etc. For information on how to obtain this book search by the title or "Books by John Stemmons" at Amazon.com. This comes automatically with a paperback binding.

440 pages $88.00

NJ-09 NEW JERSEY TAX RATABLES, 1790 [1785-1794] This book contains 2307 names of those who are taxable. Unfortunately, Burlington and Cape May counties are not covered by this period. We are fortunate though in have the petitions that cover the same time. It is interesting to compare the two sets of records. They were not combined because that would make the books too large. The tax ratables do include important details about the property they held and may provide clues regarding relationship, etc. For information on how to obtain this book search by the title or "Books by John Stemmons" at Amazon.com. This comes automatically with a paperback binding.

268 pages $53.60

NJ-10 NEW JERSEY TAX RATABLES, 1800 [1795-1804] , Volumes 1-2 This book contains 8396 names of those who are taxable. It includes important details about the property they held and may provide clues regarding relationship, etc. For information on how to obtain this book search by the title or "Books by John Stemmons" at Amazon.com. This comes automatically with a paperback binding.

Volume 1, A Through K, pages 456 $91.20
Volume 2, L Through Z, pages 449 $89.80

NC-01 NORTH CAROLINA PETITIONERS, ETC. 1780 [1775-1784]© Compiled by John Stemmons, 2021. This book contains 4866 names and was assembled from records located at the North Carolina State Archives. This was before the federal census was taken and is a valuable resource for locating people in this early time. Included are some names from what is now, Tennessee. For information on how to obtain this book search by the title or "Books by John Stemmons" at Amazon.com. This comes automatically with a paperback binding.

- Economic issues regarding the devaluation of currency, public debt, etc.
- Issues on religion and churches.
- Issues regarding counties and towns, etc.
- Issues regarding hunting on private property, fishing, etc.
- Issues about roads, bridges, canals, ferries, etc.
- Seeking new legislation or repealing existing laws.
- Issues about military and government affairs and officers.
- Seeking resolution of property and land problems, etc.
- Issues about crimes, pardon, amnesty, etc.

568 pages $113.60

1009-ROWAN COUNTY, NORTH CAROLINA TAX LISTS 1758/1759, 1761, 1768, 1778, 1779© Compiled by John D and E. Diane Stemmons, 2004. This publication serves as a census for Rowan County for about three decades which includes two major conflicts, the French and Indian and Revolutionary wars. Thus, one may be able to track individuals that stayed in the county over a significant period of time. Sometimes sons and slaves are given plus other important information. These tax lists are listed alphabetically in three separate sections.

218 pages $43.60

OH-01 TERRITORY NW OF OHIO RIVER, PETITIONERS, ETC. 1790-1800 [1785-1804] (Now Ohio)© Compiled by John D Stemmons, 2021. It contains 217 names for 1790 and 3047 names for 1800. This book may include many heads of household at that time and serves as a substitute for missing or no censuses. It even incorporates the names of many native Americans. These records provide an incredible amount of information about these early people. While censuses help track people, the records this book contains are even better in some respects than the census because it helps us understand some of their personal information not recorded by a census. Some additional biographical details may be included, plus possible relationships with other family members. For information on how to obtain this book search by the title or "Books by John Stemmons" at Amazon.com. This comes automatically with a paperback binding. It includes but is not limited to petitions regarding:

- Petition of the French inhabitants of Gallipolis regarding their purchase of lands from the Scioto Company.
- Inhabitants on the Muskingum to Governor St. Clair.
- Petitions about land and issues with John Cleves Symmes.
- 1800, Population Schedules, Washington County. Territory Northwest of the River Ohio.
- Petition by inhabitants telling of losses in the "Late Indian war" and their inability to obtain land in Kentucky.
- Petition by inhabitants of Hamilton County seeking approval to purchase reserved land in order to build a grist mill because it has a sufficient stream of water.
- List of Gallipolis proprietors and the amount of their land purchases.

285 pages $57.00

PA-01 PENNSYLVANIA CHESTER COUNTY TAX LIST 1771© Compiled by John D Stemmons, 2021. It contains 5621 names. This record lists all taxable people in the county, and as such, is a good census substitute. It is not known what is meant by the abbreviations or "inmate". Perhaps they were incarcerated in jail or were indentured in some way. Often an occupation is listed. Occasionally there will be information about family relationships. It is helpful that this book includes the information about the taxable property. For information on how to obtain this book search by the title or "Books by John Stemmons" at Amazon.com. This comes automatically with a paperback binding.

399 pages $79.80

South Carolina

South Carolina has a remarkable series of records that makes it unique for the Colonial period. These are the "Jury Lists" compiled by the government to function as a list of names from which members of a jury could be assigned. They cover the period 1720-1783 and, according to the act in 1731, were compiled from tax lists of the preceding year [which no longer exist], listing every person who paid a tax of twenty shillings or more. Those who paid five pounds or more were listed as grand jurors. The poorer class of people would not be listed. While not a complete list of the heads of household, they represent a sizeable proportion. They serve as a census during a period of growth, migration, and war. Usually only the name is given, but sometimes an occupation or name of the father is listed, etc. Many names are on more than one list for a particular year.

1010-SOUTH CAROLINA 1720 JURY LIST© Compiled by John D and E. Diane Stemmons, 2004. This publication has 840 entries covering a time when South Carolina was only 50 years old and the population was very small with only an estimated 885 heads of household. Unfortunately, it does not list a residence other than South Carolina. For information on how to obtain this book search by the title or "Books by John Stemmons" at Amazon.com. This comes automatically with a paperback binding.

48 pages $9.60

1017-SOUTH CAROLINA 1731 JURY LIST© Compiled by John D and E. Diane Stemmons, 2005. This book contains 2160 entries. It lists the locality of every person. For information on how to obtain this book search by the title or "Books by John Stemmons" at Amazon.com. This comes automatically with a paperback binding.

110 pages $22.00

1011-SOUTH CAROLINA 1740 JURY LIST© Compiled by John D and E. Diane Stemmons, 2004. This book contains 2160 entries. It lists the locality of every person. For information on how to obtain this book search by the title or "Books by John Stemmons" at Amazon.com. This comes automatically with a paperback binding.

111 pages $22.20

1012-SOUTH CAROLINA 1751 JURY LIST© Compiled by John D and E. Diane Stemmons, 2004. This book contains 2170 entries. It lists the locality of every person. For information on how to obtain this book search by the title or "Books by John Stemmons" at Amazon.com. This comes automatically with a paperback binding.

109 pages $21.80

1013-SOUTH CAROLINA 1757 JURY LIST© Compiled by John D and E. Diane Stemmons, 2004. This book contains 2624 entries. It lists the locality of every person. For information on how to obtain this book search by the title or "Books by John Stemmons" at Amazon.com. This comes automatically with a paperback binding.

135 pages $27.00

1014-SOUTH CAROLINA 1767 JURY LIST© Compiled by John D and E. Diane Stemmons, 2004. This book contains 2385 entries. It lists the locality of every person. For information on how to obtain this book search by the title or "Books by John Stemmons" at Amazon.com. This comes automatically with a paperback binding.

127 pages $25.40

SC-07 SOUTH CAROLINA 1780 [1775-1784], VOLUMES 1-2© Compiled by John D Stemmons, 2021. It contains 13,444 names. This record of jury lists consist of many people during the Colonial/Revolutionary War period and as such, is a good census substitute. Since Loyalists owned property that they paid taxes on, they may be included as well. These records provide a place of residence which can lead to other records to search. For information on how to obtain this book search by the title or "Books by John Stemmons" at Amazon.com. This comes automatically with a paperback binding.

Volume 1, 502 pages $100.40
Volume 2, 575 pages $115.00

TN-01 TENNESSEE PETITIONS, ETC., 1770-1790 [1765-1794]© Also known as Territory South of Ohio River. Compiled by John Stemmons, 2021. This book was assembled from *Territorial Papers of the United States* and contains 1 name for 1770, 12 names for 1780, and 1161 names for 1790. These people listed seem to be the more prominent persons, so, most of the less noteworthy individuals would not be listed. Still, the people listed clarify this early time before Tennessee became a state. The amount of biographical information is significant compared to the other books we have compiled from *Territorial Papers of the United States*. Many Native American names are included. For information on how to obtain this book search by the title or "Books by John Stemmons" at Amazon.com. This comes automatically with a paperback binding. It includes but is not limited to petitions regarding:

- "One of twelve men selected by the Cumberland people to govern the settlement, 1783; appointed by the Governor of North Carolina judge of the courts, Davidson County, 1783.
- Appointments about military and local officers, etc.
- Name on the "Treaty of Holston", 2 Jul 1791 between the President of the US and "Chiefs and Warriors of the Cherokee Nation of Indians."

- Memorial, 1 Aug 1791, to the President from the civil and military officers of Mero District explaining recent depredations of the Indians and seeking an "Act of Cession" from North Carolina.

95 pages $19.00

TN-02 TENNESSEE PETITIONERS, ETC. AND GRAINGER COUNTY TAX LISTS 1800 [1795-1804]© Compiled by John Stemmons, 2021. Also known as Territory South of Ohio River. This book was assembled from Grainger County Tax Lists 1800 and *Territorial Papers of the United States* and contains 182 names for the *Papers* and 247 names for the tax lists. From *Territorial Papers of the United States* the names mostly seem to be persons appointed to official or military positions or are members of the Knoxville Convention. Thus, they seem to be the more prominent persons, so, most of the less noteworthy individuals would not be listed. Still, the people listed clarify this early time before Tennessee became a state. The tax lists record the names of those who are taxable and are much more inclusive. They do include important details about the property they held. For information on how to obtain this book search by the title or "Books by John Stemmons" at Amazon.com. This comes automatically with a paperback binding. It includes but is not limited to petitions regarding:
- List, 21 Dec 1795, of members of Knoxville Convention.
- Appointments of military and local officers, etc.

49 pages $9.80

TN-03 TENNESSEE GRAINGER COUNTY TAX LISTS 1810 [1805-1814]© Compiled by John Stemmons, 2021. This book was assembled from Grainger County Tax Lists 1810 and contains 1242 names of those who are taxable. They do include important details about the property they held and may provide clues regarding relationship, etc. For information on how to obtain this book search by the title or "Books by John Stemmons" at Amazon.com. This comes automatically with a paperback binding.

146 pages $29.20

TN-04 TENNESSEE GRAINGER COUNTY TAX LISTS 1820 [1815-1824]© Compiled by John Stemmons, 2021. This book was assembled from Grainger County Tax Lists 1820 and contains 1161 names of those who are taxable. They do include important details about the property they held and may provide clues regarding relationship, etc. The lists for 1800-1820 furnish an excellent opportunity to track the population growth of the county. For information on how to obtain this book search by the title or "Books by John Stemmons" at Amazon.com. This comes automatically with a paperback binding.

131 pages $26.20

VA-01 VIRGINIA PERSONAL PROPERTY TAX LISTS, 1780 [1775-1784] (Accomack and Albemarle Counties)© Compiled by John Stemmons, 2021. This book was assembled from Accomack and Albemarle Counties Personal Property Tax Lists ca 1780 and contains 2553 names of those who are taxable. They do include important details about the property they held and may provide clues regarding relationship, etc. They even furnish the entry for, it is assumed, future president Thomas Jefferson! For information on how to obtain this book search by the title or "Books by John Stemmons" at Amazon.com. This comes automatically with a paperback binding.

252 pages $50.40

VA-02 VIRGINIA PERSONAL PROPERTY TAX LISTS, 1790 [1785-1794] (Accomack and Albemarle Counties)© Compiled by John Stemmons, 2021. This book was assembled from Accomack and Albemarle Counties Personal Property Tax Lists ca 1790 and contains 2679 names of those who are taxable, plus 3 from *Territorial Papers of the U.S.* They do include important details about the property they held and may provide clues regarding relationship, etc. They even furnish the entry for, it is assumed, future president Thomas Jefferson! Data on the age range of males is also included. For information on how to obtain this book search by the title or "Books by John Stemmons" at Amazon.com. This comes automatically with a paperback binding.

333 pages $66.60

VA-03 VIRGINIA PERSONAL PROPERTY TAX LISTS, ca 1800 [1795-1804] (Accomack and Albemarle Counties)© Compiled by John Stemmons, 2021. This book was assembled from Accomack and Albemarle Counties Personal Property Tax Lists ca 1800 and contains 3788 names of those who are taxable. They do include important details about the property they held and may provide clues regarding relationship, etc. They even furnish the entry for, it is assumed, future president Thomas Jefferson! Data on the age range of males is also included. With the lists for 1780-1800 one can track population growth in these countries. An individual showing up for the first time may indicate potential age. For information on how to obtain this book search by the title or "Books by John Stemmons" at Amazon.com. This comes automatically with a paperback binding.

436 pages $87.20

Population estimates were obtained from U.S. Bureau of the Census, *Historical Statistics of the United States, Colonial Times to 1957,* Washington, D.C., 1960, Library of Congress Card No. A 60-9150; and United States. Bureau of the Census, *A Century of Population Growth From the First Census of the United States to the Twelfth, 1790-1900* Washington: Government Printing Office, 1909. A household size of 5.7 persons was assumed.

Good morning.
We received the gift book of "Georgia Petitions 1785-1794". Fantastic book and a great tool in researching that time period. I like the format which is easy to read and puts in one place the petitions for research. I personally have searched many of the petitions and love this new tool. The introduction and the list of petitions gives much added information to understanding the petitions for the various individuals.
I look forward to ordering more books in July after our budget is in place. Thank you for contacting our library and making us aware of your fine publications. Have a great day.
Thanks,
Irene Godwin
Ellen Payne Odom Genealogy Library
204 5th St. S.E.
P.O. Box 2828
Moultrie, GA 31768

EXAMPLES OF THE KIND OF INFORMATION CONTAINED IN OUR BOOKS

Cicotte, J. Bte., Michigan Territory, District of Detroit, "Cote des Poux"

Cicotte, J. Bte.,	45-Over?	Male	**Color:**	White
10-16		Male	**Color:**	White
10-16		Male	**Color:**	White
16-26		Male	**Color:**	White

45-Over   Female   **Color:**   White
1810 Census of the District of Detroit
MS/Witherell (B. F. H.) Collection, LMS, Burton Historical Collection, Detroit Public Library, Folder 2
Cicotte, Jacques,   Michigan Territory
           Cicotte, Jacques,   Male
Petition, 26 Oct 1807, to Congress from inhabitants of Michigan Ter. seeking time to file claims to their land, claims on 1+ parcels be confirmed, farms on Detroit River be extended to 80 arpents, & occupancy later than 1 Jul 1796 be allowed [pp. 138-49].
Territorial Papers of the US - volume: 10 page: 146
Holeday, Jas,   Territory NW of Ohio River   Knox County, Vincennes
           Holeday, Jas,   Male
Address to Colonel Josiah Harmar by American inhabitants of Post Vincennes dated 4 Aug 1787
Territorial Papers of US - volume: 2 page: 65
Holliday, Heirs of James,   Territory NW of Ohio River   Knox County, Vincennes
           Holliday, Heirs of James,   Male
Petition, 7 Aug 1797, to Congress by inhabitants of Knox County, who migrated to Vincennes around 1786 and received land, but never obtained a deed.
Territorial Papers of US - volume: 2 page: 621
Lajoye, Pierre ,   Spanish North America, St. Louis
           Lajoye, Pierre,   Male
"Pierre Lajoye, formerly of Prairie du Rocher on the American side of the Mississippi".
Letter, 1790, by Governor St. Clair to Manuel Perez concerning an American boy in the possession of Pierre Lajoye [pages 237-238].
"Mr. Mayet has just complained to me that a Mr. La Joye, to whom he has entrusted an American boy, whom he took from the savages, to be returned to the parents of the latter, has not returned him, but is holding the boy as a slave and refuses to return the boy to them on the pretext of some debt. I am convinced that you will not find it proper that a free child should be held as a slave for the debts of another--and will order Mr. La Joye to return him to Mayet."
Letter, 26 May 1790, from St. Louis by Manuel Perez to Governor St. Clair concerning an American boy in the possession of Pierre Lajoye [pages 237-240]:
"MY DEAR SIR: In order to take cognizance of the subject of the claim in your favor of the 20th instant concerning the child who is today in the possession of Mr. Lajoye, I had the latter appear before me and from the questions which I put to him and the reasons which he advanced to me on this subject I have found in him only a disposition to render service to the Unhappy Father who lost him and who asks for him in a letter of which the said Mr. Lajoye is the bearer.
     After studying this matter carefully, I find that the above-mentioned child claimed by Mr. Mayet can leave the possession of Mr. Lajoye only to go to that of the Father now living at Natches. I think also that it is just for the said Mr. Mayet to be reimbursed for what he actually gave the savages in order to get him out of their barbarous hands; . . .
     When the young man arrived at Mr. Lajoye's house, he came and notified me of it at once and that he would write to the lower part of the Colony to learn in what district the Father of the said child lived. He learned later from the letter of which he is the bearer, that he resides at Natchez; accordingly he will send him down on the first opportunity."
Territorial Papers of the US - volume: 2 page: 237
Mayfield, Geddeon, Kentucky Barren County
           Mayfield, Geddeon,   Male
Acres of land: 200; Barren Co.; watercourse: Mill Creek; Entry: Geddeon Mayfield; Survey: same; Patent: 0; white males over 21: 0; white males 16-21: 0; blacks over 16: 0; total blacks: 0; horses: 0; stud horses: 0; retail stores: 0; tavern license: 0.
Barren County Tax Book, 1800, part 1 - page: 10 FAMILY HISTORY LIBRARY film 7865

<hr>

LEGISLATIVE PETITIONS

Petitions to the governor, legislature, etc., were a particularly important way for individuals to communicate with their government regarding issues that were very essential to them. Their influence in making changes throughout our history has contributed to making our society what it is today. They are an important link in our legislative and judicial history. In these early petitions one can trace the growing desire for democracy. In fact, they are one of the most visible manifestations of democracy in practice. It is fascinating to view the changes in the reasons for submitting petitions over time (see the lists below.)

Because petitions represent the feelings of one or more individuals, they provide a window into the soul of the petitioners that illuminates the historical landscape. Most aspects of the human condition are addressed in some form by these important documents. The names listed with the petition can be used as a census of inhabitants for a particular locality. Often it is possible to determine useful information about individual persons from these records. They can help compensate for lost or destroyed county records. Petitions are original records that contain historical background about our culture and society.

Unfortunately, petitions are among the most inaccessible and underused records because there are so many, they are often difficult and time-consuming to read, and are usually housed only in the state archives or other repository in their un-microfilmed condition.

To help resolve this problem, we have abstracted the content of many petitions and indexed the names of the petitioners. A brief context of the petition is provided with each name. Generally, we have not included those petitions with fewer than 10-12 names.

GENEALOGY AND LOCAL HISTORY BOOKS IN PDF FORMAT ON A FLASH DRIVE

705 Local and Family History books for $75-or 11 cents a book!!! All 4 volumes of Savage's Genealogical Dictionary of New England would cost you about $0.44!*
You can have in your library/home more books of this type than most libraries have. They cover nearly all aspects of human experience including law, medicine, biography, history, etc., etc.

Concerns?
1. **Question:** I am uncomfortable in letting patrons use this small drive as it may become lost.
   Answer: Simply download the contents of the drive onto your computer(s) and keep the drive in a safe place. We will replace it at no charge if it becomes lost.
2. **Question:** Some of our books, including those on microfilm, that are also on your flash drive are in poor condition because of patron use through the years, especially when copies are made. Copies made from microfilm are not always the best quality. How can you help us with these problems?
   Answer: Once our books are on your computers, your originals can be kept in a secured area so that no more damage will occur because of hands-on use. The images on the computer can be easily printed, usually with better quality.
3. **Question:** We are only interested in items covering the locality our patrons live in.
   Answer: Many of your patrons were born outside of your area and/or have ancestry from all over the United States, etc.
4. **Question:** Are these books under copyright restrictions?
   Answer: They are in the public domain and so are not copyrightable.

Approximately how many pages do the 705 books add up to?
Total cost (from Stemmons Publishing) for hard copies: $7044 (not available now)
Approximated total pages of text on the flash drive: 221,307
Approximated total images on the flash drive: 58,272

A huge genealogical library of 705 books on your computer for only $75
A dealer's discount is available of $45 for 5 or more flash drives.
Imagine 705 books… 60,417 images… 230,642 pages on a small flash drive.

You may be able to find these books on Google, Ancestry, or FamilySearch. To make a hard copy from these sources may be expensive, especially if you were to copy all 705! I may be mistaken, but I'm not sure you can print just a single page from those services. You can with my books. You also have them immediately at your fingertips without needing to go to the effort to search these other services.
The downside to these books is that many are not indexed.
No problem: just check the index provided by these other sources before using our books.
"In 2016, popular genealogy blogger Dick Eastman surmised that perhaps ninety percent of the resources you may need to fill out your family tree are not yet available on the Internet." This statement was found on the Boston Public Library website. If that is true, some of the books on our flash drive may not be found on the Internet.

You may obtain a copy of the drive by sending check, money order, or cash to John Stemmons at 1078 Shields Lane, South Jordan, Utah, 801-254-2152 (Call between 9:00 a.m. and 5:00 p.m. Monday through Friday. If no one answers, please leave a message.), stemmonspublishing@gmail.com. We have been in this business since 1975! Check BBB if you need to.

The fee for shipping and handling is $10.00 unless you send a shipping container, deliverable to you, with sufficient postage to mail to you. Please allow 4-6 weeks for delivery.

The books on the drive are in the public domain and are not copyrighted. You may make as many copies of them as you would like. Please do not place the contents of the drive, in part or in full, on the Internet except for individual pages.

We do not do credit cards and PayPal. If you are unhappy with the drive, please return it for a refund of your money.

If you would like a list of questions and answers or a list of the books, please let us know.

*How are we able to do this? Simply by reducing each page so that 2-6 pages can be placed on a single 8½ by 11 sheet of paper and still be readable. With the computer, you can enlarge it as many times as needed.

Number of books by locality:
US-99, Regional-32, AL-1, CT-31, DE-1, GA-2, IL-1, IN-1, KY-1, ME-23, MD-15, MA-91, MI-1, MN-1, MO-2, NH-20, NJ-28, NY-81, NC-9, OH-9, PA-51, RI-6, SC-26, VT-2, VA-47, WV-1; Family History-62; CN-5; EN-39; IR-10; SCOT-7=705 books!

www.ingramcontent.com/pod-product-compliance
Lightning Source LLC
Chambersburg PA
CBHW080244260726
48658CB00008B/3229